# The Secret Destiny
## of America

# OTHER BOOKS BY MANLY PALMER HALL

The theme and pattern for this book was first developed in a lecture given by the author at Carnegie Hall, New York, December 2, 1942. An aroused public interest in the subject led to further research with enlargement of the findings and this publication in book form.

# THE SECRET DESTINY
# OF AMERICA

## BY MANLY PALMER HALL 1901-

FIRST EDITION

45-1053

PHILOSOPHICAL RESEARCH SOCIETY

3341 Griffith Park Boulevard — Los Angeles 27, Calif.

# Descriptive Contents

## 1

### THE ORIGIN OF THE DEMOCRATIC IDEAL

World democracy was the secret dream of the great classical philosophers....Thousands of years before Columbus they were aware of the existence of our Western Hemisphere and selected it to be the site of the philosophic empire....The brilliant plan of the Ancients has survived to our time, and it will continue to function until the great work is accomplished....The American nation desperately needs a vision of its own purpose....... *page 15*

## 2

### THE WORLD'S FIRST DEMOCRAT

The leader who had the first social consciousness in the administration of a nation was a Pharaoh of Egypt, Akhnaton....Born several thousand years too soon, he was the first realist in democracy, the first humanitarian, the first internationalist....He saw that the duty of the ruler is to protect for all the right to live well, to think, to dream, to hope, and to aspire....For his dream of the Brotherhood of Man he cheerfully gave his life....*page 27*

## 3

### WESTWARD OCEAN TRAVEL TO THE EARTHLY PARADISE

From Plutarch's description of voyages it can be calculated that our great continent in the Western Hemisphere was visited by the ancient Greeks; they not only reached our shores but explored part of the Great Lakes area.... Under a thin veil of symbolism they perpetuated in mythology their knowledge of our land, which they called blessed....The area was anciently set apart for coming generations in the great human experiment of the democratic commonwealth ........................ *page 36*

# 4

## THE FIRST ELECTION OF LAW-MAKERS

Solon, of Athens, freed the debtor's person to reform the institution of debt slavery; he instituted the selection of juries by lot, with all citizens participating; and he gave the voting franchise to all taxpayers alike, thus beginning national democracy six hundred years before Christ.... When he later journeyed to Egypt, he there learned of the first war of conquest, in the story of the lost Atlantis, and became acquainted with the imperishable laws for the government of nations

# 5

## THE ANCIENT LEAGUE OF NATIONS

A description of the lost Atlantis was written by Plato; it introduces the league formed by the ten benevolent kings who ruled the lesser nations and the three great continents of Europe, Asia, and Africa; and who bound themselves by oath to obey the divine laws of enduring empire....This was the philosophic democracy, with all men having the right to become wise through self-discipline and self-improvement, thus achieving the only aristocracy recognized by Natural Law....The Atlantis story continues to the later decision of the kings to use their united power to enslave all the peoples of the earth, and the consequent destruction of Atlantis by earthquake and fire....Interpreted politically, it is the story of the breaking up of the ideal pattern of government

# 6

## A ROMAN PROJECT TO GIVE RULERSHIP TO THE WISE

The Platonic point of view was envisioned by Plotinus to take form as a philosophers' city, establishment of which was approved by his Roman emperor as the noblest experiment in time....But the fear of the Roman Senators that the projected commonwealth of learning might finally overthrow the empire brought the project to naught, as Rome continued in the advanced state of smugness that immediately preceded the complete collapse of the nation .....................................

# 7

## THE DEMOCRATIC TRADITION PRESERVED BY SECRET SOCIETIES

For more than three thousand years, secret societies have labored to create the background of knowledge necessary to the establishment of an enlightened democracy among the nations of the world....The Greek Dionysians were social and political temple builders, known as the Collegians in later Rome....The rise of the Christian Church brought persecution of the classical intellectual pattern's ideology, driving the guilds into greater secrecy; but all have continued searching for human happiness under a variety of rituals and symbols; and they still exist, as the Order of the Quest........................

# 8

## A NEW IDENTITY FOR CHRISTOPHER COLUMBUS

Many scholars were fully aware of the global form of the earth in the time of Columbus, who, according to early historians, State documents, and his own son, was not an Italian of humble station and uneducated, but was a Greek Prince with an excellent classical education....It was from a Greek port that he sailed on the celebrated voyage of discovery. He was accompanied by a mysterious stranger, which has suggested that Columbus was an agent of the society of unknown philosophers....The pattern of the democratic ideal was beginning to assert itself over the tyranny of decadent aristocracy. A new world was necessary for a new idea....When it was necessary, it was discovered ...............................

# 9

## THE PROPHECIES OF NOSTRADAMUS

Eleven years after Columbus reached our shores, an extraordinary man was born in France. In adult life he was both a respected physician and a mystic who was able to write accurately the history of the world to come.... There was no indication at the time that in the Western Hemisphere would arise a great nation, but Dr. Michel Nostradamus saw a civilization established there that would observe (always on a Thursday) a day to express thanksgiving for freedom of religion, freedom of opportunity, and freedom of life....He prophesied that this nation would free itself from the bonds of the mother country, would greatly prosper, but would have to fight several wars—one with the Orient—before becoming a great power in a pattern of world peace, with other nations looking to it for leadership....All that he foretold is precisely according to the Platonic tradition.....

# 10

## THE DESIGN OF UTOPIAS

Sir Thomas More wrote a fable, about four hundred years ago, to set forth the social state of man in a philosophic commonwealth, but so completely has the world missed the entire point, that the very word "Utopia" is even today a synonym for optimistic but impractical ideals of reform. ....Campenella, an Italian philosopher, wrote of the major tragedy in that the subject of statesmanship had alone been neglected as practically every other subject had been reduced to a science. Government officials, he insisted, should be elected after examination to determine knowledge and fitness....Boccalini contributed further to Utopian literature, and Andreae sought to Christianize it with the theme: "For lack of vision the people perish.".

# 11

## THE OBJECTIVE OF THE SECRET SOCIETY

One reference to a secret society in Bacon's *New Atlantis* is scarcely less than a proclamation of the Society of

Unknown Philosophers but has gone unnoticed for three hundred years....This fable is of the land of Bensalem, meaning the Son of Peace, which with its merchandise, the Light of Truth, maintained a trade with Atlantis, which was declared to be the same as America....Everything indicates that it was Sir Francis Bacon's dream that the enlarging of the bounds of human empire should be instituted on our own continent, an area peculiarly set aside by Nature for the perfection of philosophy and the sciences ............................................. *page 108*

# 12

## WESTERN CULTURE A THOUSAND YEARS BEFORE COLUMBUS

In the Mexican area the civilization then existing was the most advanced on the earth....The ancient Mayas had massive public buildings and observatories in at least a hundred cities, and these were connected by broad paved highways. Rulers were elected by the common agreement of the people. The Mayas hold the world record for a continued peace of five hundred years; this has been attributed to their having possessed no monetary symbol or curency for goods exchange. Theirs was the first democratic State on a continent set aside for the perfection of the dream of democracy....Long before the coming of the white man, the spirit of human equality, human cooperation, and freedom of worship had flourished here ................................................. *page 117*

# 13

## BACON'S SECRET SOCIETY IS SET UP IN AMERICA

Men bound by a secret oath to labor in the cause of world democracy decided that in the American colonies they would plant the roots of a new way of life. Brotherhoods were established to meet secretly, and they quietly and industriously conditioned America to its destiny for leadership in a free world....Benjamin Franklin exercised an enormous psychological influence in Colonial politics as the appointed spokesman of the unknown philosophers; he did not make laws, but his words became law. *page 126*

# 14

## A PROPHECY WRITTEN IN THE YEAR OF WASHINGTON'S BIRTH

Sir William Hope noted the birth overseas of an infant starred by fate to rule both freemen and slaves, and named the year of the American Declaration of Independence forty-four years before it was signed. He gave in Cabalistic form the patriot leader's name, and the years of his lifetime span....The prophecy also singled out Abraham Lincoln, designated the term of Benjamin Harrison as the one to mark the first century of the new nation's progress....It is a reasonable assumption that the Hope prophecy is a genuine example of foreknowledge of the destiny of the United States ................. *Page 135*

# 15

## THE UNKNOWN MAN WHO DESIGNED OUR FLAG

Our flag was worked out in elements of design that provided for gradual modification in the future as the national destiny increased. It was a learned stranger, added by seeming accident to the committee appointed by the Colonial Congress in 1775, who had the foresight to provide the area for the stars in subsequent substitution for the British Union Jack. The design was adopted by General Washington; there is no record that the committee ever made a report to Congress....According to the rules laid down by Sir Francis Bacon for works published under the authority of the society of unknown philosophers, each book must be so marked as to be readily recognizable. The book that tells of the presence of the unknown designer ends with a quotation from Bacon....... *page 146*

# 16

## THOMAS PAINE AND THE RIGHTS
## OF MAN

The crusading of Tom Paine definitely advanced for Americans that secret destiny by which all people shall be free and equal. There is little doubt that he assisted Jefferson in writing the Declaration of Independence.... Paine emphasized the necessity of separating the spheres of Church and State in government, preached religious tolerance in a day when the spirit of persecution was still strong, attacked the special privileges of the aristocracy... Only by thousands of years of conditioning can mankind be brought to the perfectionist state envisioned by this American patriot .......................... *page 155*

# 17

## THE UNKNOWN WHO SWAYED THE SIGNERS
## OF THE DECLARATION OF INDEPENDENCE

Faced with the death penalty for high treason, courageous men debated long before they picked up the quill pen to sign the parchment that declared the independence of the colonies from the mother country. For many hours they had debated in the State House at Philadelphia, with the lower chamber doors locked and a guard posted—when suddenly a voice rang out from the balcony. A burst of eloquence to the keynote, "God has given America to be free!" ended with the delegates rushing forward to sign. ...The American patriots then turned to express their gratitude to the unknown speaker. The speaker was not in the balcony; he was not to be found anywhere. How he entered and left the locked and guarded room is not known. No one knows to this day who he was.. *page 164*

# 18

## THE SYMBOLS OF THE GREAT SEAL
## OF THE U. S.

Is the American eagle actually a Phoenix? Selection of the fabulous bird of the ancients seems to have been the intention of the designer of our nation's Great Seal. The Phoenix is the symbol of the Reborn in Wisdom.... The design on the reverse of the Great Seal is even more definitely related to the Order of the Quest. The pyramid and the all-seeing eye represent the Universal House surmounted by the radiant emblem of the Great Architect of the Universe.... These three symbols appearing in combination is more than chance or coincidence..... *page 173*

## 19

### THE PROPHETIC DREAM OF GENERAL MC CLELLAN

In a dark hour of military apprehension the General of the Union forces was visited by a vision in a dream. A voice spoke and a map came alive with troop movements as the enemy forces moved into the very positions he had intended to occupy. The voice told him he had been betrayed; he raised his eyes and looked into the face of George Washington.... When Mc Clellan awoke his map was covered with marks and signs and figures, indicating the strategy that prevented the capture of the nation's Capitol.... Also included in the dream was the warning of the Father of Our Country that we would wage still another struggle for existence "ere another century shall have gone by" against the "oppressors of the whole earth." ...................................... *page 182*

## 20

### THE END OF THE QUEST

In America shall be erected a shrine to Universal Truth, as here arises the global democratic Commonwealth—the true wealth of all mankind, which is designed in the foundation that men shall abide together in peace and shall devote their energies to the common cause of discovery.... The power of man lies in his dreams, his visions, and his ideals. This has been the common vision of man's necessity in the secret empire of the Brotherhood of the Quest, consecrated to fulfilling the destiny for which we in America were brought into being.. *page 191*

# 1

## THE ORIGIN OF THE DEMOCRATIC IDEAL

World democracy was the secret dream of the great classical philosophers.... Thousands of years before Columbus they were aware of the existence of our Western Hemisphere and selected it to be the site of the philosophic empire.... The brilliant plan of the Ancients has survived to our time, and it will continue to function until the great work is accomplished.... The American nation desperately needs a vision of its own purpose.

By preserved symbols we can know that it is from the remote past, from the deep shadows of the medieval world, as well as from the early struggles of more modern times, that the power of American democracy has come

# 1

MERICA can not refuse the challenge of leadership in the postwar world. Mere physical reconstruction of ravaged countries and the reorganization of political, economic, and social systems is the lesser task we will face. The larger problem and the great challenge is in how to set up a new order of world ethics firmly established on a foundation of democratic idealism.

Experts in various fields have already submitted programs designed to meet the needs of those nations whose way of life has been disrupted by war. But with the failing common to specially trained minds, these planners incline to think mostly in the terms of their own particular interests. As yet, no one has touched the fundamentals of international ethics. No one has advanced a working plan securely based upon a broad, deep, and sympathetic understanding of the *human being* and his problems. The thinking has been in the dual fields of power politics and material economics, with remedies expressed in terms of charts, blueprints, patterns, and industrial programs.

But, there is one new and encouraging element present in most of the recommendations of today's experts. They are recognizing the necessity of conceiving the world as one inter-dependent structure. Yet, even as they recognize the need for a unity of human interests, their recommendations are for the perpetuation of highly competitive economic policies, which, if they are consistently applied, must lead in the end to war and discord.

It is not an easy task to unite the efforts of the human race toward the accomplishment of any common good. Mankind in the majority is selfish, provincial in attitude, and concerned primarily with personal success and acquiring creature comforts. It will not be possible to build an enduring peace until the average man has been convinced that personal selfishness is detrimental to personal happiness and personal success. It must be shown that self-seeking has gone out of fashion, and that the world is moving on to a larger conception of living.

The postwar planners have more of idealism in their programs than has ever before been expressed in the problem of the relationships of nations. But it still is not enough. A clear and complete statement of a world purpose is required—a world dream great enough to inspire unity of world effort.

These are the days of America's opportunity to lead a still troubled mankind toward a better way of life. If we meet this challenge, we will insure not only survival of our nation for centuries to come, but we shall gain the enduring gratitude of our fellowmen and Americans will be remembered to the end of time as a great enlightened people.

It is not enough that we solve particular problems. We must solve the very cause of problem itself. Wars, depressions, crime, dictators and their oppressions, are the symptoms giving clear indication of a greater ailment. To examine each problem solely in terms of the problem itself, without recognition of its true relationship to a larger and more universal necessity, is to fail in the broader implications of an enduring peace and prosperity.

Experience should have taught us long ago that policies which have originated from material considerations and attitudes have proved inadequate. The whole story of civilization and the records of history tell us that all such adjustments hold no hope of lasting peace or security. But, here we are again preparing ourselves to be satisfied with temporary solutions for permanent problems.

The recognition is long overdue that we over-simplify the problem of world peace when we think that process is one of breaking the task down for examination of its materialistic parts, and then hopefully devising an applicable remedy for each of these. The physical conditions of human existence are not the whole of the human problem. We could adjust all material considerations to the point of supremest equity, and yet accomplish virtually nothing solutional.

The greatest of known problems is the human problem. And not until all embracing examination is made into every phase of human needs can there be an adequate reconstruction policy for a postwar world. That man is physical is obvious; but he is also mental, and emotional; he is spiritual, and he has a soul. These latter factors are not so obvious.

What to do about them is not so easy; for they are difficult to understand, and even more difficult to classify and reduce to a working pattern. We as builders of a civilization will have to learn that only when equal consideration is given to each of these elements of man's nature will we arrive at the solutions for the disasters into which men and nations precipitate themselves.

Our postwar reconstructors—ours, if not by our selection, at least with our consent—are not outstandingly qualified for this broader task. Few indeed are the statesmen and politicians who have any conception of man as a spiritual being. And as for military leaders, they are primarily disciplinarians, invaluable as such in times of war, but not at all emotionally geared to problems of individualistic peacetime character. And world planners recruited from among our industrial leaders, it must be admitted, are not generally informed on the workings of the human psyche. Those who have made the study of human conduct their life work, the sociologists, have little scientific knowledge of the hidden springs that animate that very conduct into its amazing diversity of manifestations. And if a word is to be said for bringing in the clergy, it might be that the theologian planner who will be truly useful will be one who acquires at least some knowledge of the science of biology.

We are displaying a woeful lack of vision in the way we fumble with the eternal laws of life. It is not enough that we now hopefully create a setup permitting men to give allegiance with their minds or to serve faithfully with their bodies. We must some day face the truth that man is inevitably and incurably an idealist; for this is the truth that will set us free. Man's need is for the idealistic content of his nature to be properly nourished; then his

whole consciousness will impel him to right action
—and then no more will our laws fail, treaties be
broken, and the rights of man stand violated.

The American nation desperately needs a vision
of its own purpose. It must conceive it in a generous idealism, great and strong enough to bind
thoughtless and selfish persons to something bigger
than themselves. It must recognize that it is in
the intangible ideal that the foundations are laid
for all seeable good, must know that the truly practical course and the course of hard realism for
America is the one that is laid basically in a generous idealism.

This is more than an indicated course. It is one
that we inevitably must follow, guided by the hand
of destiny.

Believing this to be so, I dedicate this book to
the proposition that American Democracy is part
of a Universal Plan.

Our world is ruled by inflexible laws which control not only the motions of the heavenly bodies, but
the consequences of human conduct. These Universal motions, interpreted politically, are impelling
human society out of a state of autocracy and tyranny to democracy and freedom. This motion is
inevitable, for the growth of humans is a gradual

development of mind over matter, and the motion itself represents the natural and reasonable unfoldment of the potentials within human character.

Those who attempt to resist this motion destroy themselves. To cooperate with this motion, and to assist Nature in every possible way to the accomplishment of its inevitable purpose, is to survive.

Thousands of years before the beginning of the Christian era many enlightened thinkers discovered the will of God as expressed through Nature in the affairs of men. They made known their discoveries in terms of religions, philosophies, sciences, arts, and political systems. These first statements are now the admired monuments of ancient learning. Available to men of today, they are generally ignored.

Years of research among the records of olden peoples available in libraries, museums, and shrines of ancient cultures, has convinced me that there exists in the world today, and has existed for thousands of years, a body of enlightened humans united in what might be termed, an Order of the Quest. It is composed of those whose intellectual and spiritual perceptions have revealed to them that civilization has a Secret Destiny—secret, I say, because this high purpose is not realized by the many; the great masses of peoples still live along without any knowledge whatsoever that they are part of a Universal Motion in time and space.

Pythagoras, Plato, Aristotle, Buddha, Jesus and Mohammed are among the greatest names recorded in history; but it is not customary to regard the men who bore these names as statesmen or sociologists. They are thought of as philosophers, sages, seers, and mystics, whose doctrines have no application to the political needs of an industrial civilization. Yet it is men like Plato and Buddha who still exercise the most powerful force in mortal affairs toward the perpetuation and preservation of a civilized state among all nations.

All of the great leaders of ancient times realized and taught that the establishment of a state of permanent peace among the nations depended upon the release of human ideals, but through properly trained and disciplined minds capable of interpreting these ideals in terms of the common good.

World democracy was the secret dream of the great classical philosophers. Toward the accomplishment of this greatest of all human ends they outlined programs of education, religion, and social conduct directed to the ultimate achievement of a practical and universal brotherhood. And in order to accomplish their purposes more effectively, these ancient scholars bound themselves with certain mystic ties into a broad confraternity. In Egypt, Greece, India, and China, the State Mysteries came into existence. Orders of initiated priest-philosophers were formed as a sovereign body to instruct, advise, and direct the rulers of the States.

Thousands of years ago, in Egypt, these mystical orders were aware of the existence of the western hemisphere and the great continent which we call America. The bold resolution was made that this western continent should become the site of the philosophic empire. Just when this was done it is impossible now to say, but certainly the decision was reached prior to the time of Plato, for a thinly veiled statement of this resolution is the substance of his treatise on the Atlantic Islands.

One of the most ancient of man's constructive ideals is the dream of a universal democracy and a cooperation of all nations in a commonwealth of States. The mechanism for the accomplishment of this ideal was set in motion in the ancient temples of Greece, Egypt, and India. So brilliant was the plan and so well was it administrated that it has survived to our time, and it will continue to function until the great work is accomplished.

Philosophy set up its house in the world to free men by freeing them of their own inordinate desires and ambitions. It saw selfishness as the greatest crime against the common good, for selfishness is natural to all who are untutored. It recognized that the mind has to be trained in the laws of thinking before men can be capable of self-rulership. And it knew that the democratic commonwealth can be a reality only when our world is a world of self-ruling men.

And so it is from the remote past, from the deep shadows of the medieval world as well as from the early struggles of more modern times, that the power of American democracy has come. But we are only on the threshold of the democratic state. Not only must we preserve that which we have gained through ages of striving, we must also perfect the plan of the ages, setting up here the machinery for a world brotherhood of nations and races.

This is our duty, and our glorious opportunity.

It seems to me that the basic plan for the postwar world should be one solidly founded in this great dream of Universal Brotherhood. It is not enough to work on the problem solely in terms of politics and industry. The formula must express a broad idealism, one which appeals to the finest intuitions of man, and one universally understandable by all who have lived, dreamed, and suffered on this mortal sphere.

# 2

## THE WORLD'S FIRST DEMOCRAT

The leader who had the first social consciousness in the administration of a nation was a Pharaoh of Egypt, Akhnaton....Born several thousand years too soon, he was the first realist in democracy, the first humanitarian, the first internationalist....He saw that the duty of the ruler is to protect for all the right to live well, to think, to dream, to hope, and to aspire....For his dream of the Brotherhood of Man he cheerfully gave his life.

Akhnaton, Pharaoh of Egypt, born 1388 B. C., was the
first man in recorded history to exemplify social consciousness in the administration of a great nation. He saw
every living thing as having a divine right to live well,
to hope and to aspire in a world governed by brotherly
love

# 2

AN has passed out of the state of savagery and become a civilized creature with the development of social consciousness. Civilization is a collective state. In our collective type of life the isolationist is a detriment to himself and a menace to all others.

There is a great difference between isolationism and intellectualism. Development of the mind releases the individual from mob psychology, but it does not set him apart from the common responsibilities of his kind. A true thinker becomes a force for good within the group life. If his intellectual powers lure him away from the practical problems and values of his world, he can no longer make his contribution to the social unity.

Political reforms are not accomplished by the people, but through the people. Behind all collective progress stands the enlightened individual's leadership. His superiority does not free him from common responsibility; his is the obligation to assume the greater burden of directing his vision to the well being of all his people.

Let us see how this works. We'll go far back to ancient times.

Akhnaton, Pharaoh of Egypt, throned under the title Amen-Hotep IV, is often referred to as the first civilized human being. While this may not be literally true, he was definitely the first man in recorded history to exemplify social consciousness in the administration of a great nation.

Akhnaton, the beloved child of the Aton, was born at Thebes about 1388 B. C. Like most of the princes of his house, he was extremely delicate as a child, and it was feared that he would not live to reach the throne; as the last of his line, the dynasty would end with him if he died without issue. For this reason he was married in his twelfth year to a ten year old Egyptian girl of noble birth, named Nefertiti.

During the childhood of the young king, the Queen mother, Tiy, ruled as regent of the double empire. She is believed to have been of Syrian origin, which would account for the many strange and un-Egyptian ideas in religion, government and art which were developed during the reign of

Akhnaton. Queen Tiy, brilliant and capable, had recognized before her son reached his majority that in him were qualities more divine than human. The son became the actual ruler of his country in his eighteenth year; his reign extended for seventeen years.

Akhnaton had been ruler of Egypt only about two years when he opposed his will to the priesthood of Amon-Ra. By attacking the oldest and most firmly established of all Egyptian institutions, the young Pharaoh created legions of enemies and brought down upon himself the wrath of the religion of the State. He could scarcely have chosen a surer way of complicating the problems of his life.

In the midst of this conflict he proclaimed a new spiritual dispensation, and to escape his enemies built a new capitol city, one hundred and sixty miles up the Nile from Cairo. His new faith was Atonism; and he named his city Khut-en-Aton— the Horizon of the Aton—and dedicated the city with these words: "Ye behold the City of the Horizon of Aton, which the Aton has desired me to make for Him as a monument, in the great name of My Majesty forever. For it was Aton, my Father, that brought me to this City of the Horizon."

As High Priest of his new religion, Amen-Hotep IV changed his name to Akhnaton, because the older name included the word Amen, whose faith he had rejected.

Charles F. Potter, in his *History of Religion,* says of Akhnaton that he was, "the first pacifist, the first realist, the first monotheist, the first democrat, the first heretic, the first humanitarian, the first internationalist, and the first person known to attempt to found a religion. He was born out of due time, several thousand years too soon."

From his twenty-sixth year to his thirty-first year, Akhnaton devoted his life to the perfection of his mystical doctrine in the city which he had built for the Ever Living God. Here he taught the mystery of the Divine Father, and wrote the simple and beautiful poems which have endured and survived time. To Akhnaton, God was not a mighty warrior ruling over Egypt, speaking through the oracles of his priests; he was not a Supreme Being flying through the air in a war chariot leading armies of destruction. Aton was the gentle father who loved all his children, of every race and nation; and desired for them that they should live together in peace and comradeship.

Even more, God, the Aton, had created all the lesser creatures, whether birds that nested in the papyrus reeds along the banks of the Nile, or dragonflies with many colored wings that hovered over quiet pools and the lotus blooms. The Aton was the father of all beasts, and fishes, and flowers, and insects. He had fashioned them in his wisdom and preserved them with his love and tenderness.

Akhnaton, seated in the garden of his palace, spent many hours watching the flight of birds and listening to the voices of little creatures. He tells us that he found the Aton in all of them; and that his heart went out to them, and he gave thanks for the goodness in everything that lived.

This was a Pharaoh who traveled alone through the countryside, meeting the peasants, conversing with slaves, and sharing the simple food of the poor. To the most ignorant man he listened with profound respect, for in each of his subjects he sought and found the life of the Aton. He saw the Universal God shining through the eyes of little children, beheld the beauty of the Aton in the bodies of the men who worked in the fields. He could not understand why others did not see God in everything, as he did.

Like most of the great religious leaders, Akhnaton accepted the social problem of life as part of religion. He could not accept the inequalities of birth, wealth, or physical estate as a justification for men persecuting each other or exploiting one another. He saw every living thing having a divine right—a right to live well, to think, to dream, to hope, and to aspire. He saw it the duty of the ruler to protect this beauty in the hearts of his people, to nourish it, and to give every possible opportunity for its expression and perfection.

Religious intolerance was impossible among those who worshipped the Aton, and there was no room for political intolerance in a world governed by the laws of brotherly love. Each man became the protector and comforter of all other men, cherishing the dreams of others equally with his own.

In his personal life Akhnaton emerges as the first man in history to bring dignity and gentle beauty to the management of his home. He was the father of seven daughters, to whom he was completely devoted, and in his speeches and public pronouncements he always referred to Queen Nefertiti as "my beloved wife."

It was usual for the Pharaohs to cause themselves to be depicted in great stone carvings upon the walls of their palaces. They were represented as majestic figures, crowned and sceptered; they were shown either seated on their thrones or wielding their weapons against their foes. Akhnaton was the only Pharaoh in the history of Egypt who chose to be depicted with his arm about his wife, with his little daughters playing about and seated on his lap.

As with the passing years the health of the
Pharaoh grew worse, the opposition of the priesthood of Amon-Ra grew greater; and his reign was
complicated by invasions by the Hittite nations.
The governors of various provinces pleaded with
him for help, but Akhnaton would not send armies.

The dreamer king saw his lands pillaged and his
cities conquered; but he would not kill his enemies; they, too, were children of the Aton.

Akhnaton died in his thirty-sixth year, at the altar
of the Aton in the temple of the faith he had created.

When his mummy case was found, the following prayer to the Aton was discovered inscribed on
golden foil beneath his feet. "I breathe the sweet
breath which comes forth from Thy mouth. I
behold Thy beauty every day.... Give me Thy
hands, holding Thy spirit, that I may receive it
and may be lifted by it. Call Thou upon my
name unto eternity, and it shall never fail."

In the words of the great Egyptologist, Professor
Breasted, "There died with him such a spirit as the
world had never seen before."

Akhnaton was the first man in history who dared
to dream of the Brotherhood of Men, and he cheerfully gave his life and his empire for that dream.

He is indeed, "The beautiful child of the Living
Aton, whose name shall live forever and ever."

# 3

## WESTWARD OCEAN TRAVEL TO THE
## EARTHLY PARADISE

From Plutarch's description of voyages it can be calculated that our great continent in the Western Hemisphere was visited by the ancient Greeks; they not only reached our shores but explored part of the Great Lakes area.... Under a thin veil of symbolism they perpetuated in mythology their knowledge of our land, which they called blessed....The area was anciently set apart for coming generations in the great human experiment of the democratic commonwealth.

THE ancient Greeks had a far better knowledge of geography than popular opinion today indicates. We have been deceived as to the full measure of classical learning, because the Greeks did not commit the larger part of their knowledge to writing, and they bound scholarship with the vow of secrecy.

In ancient days all learning was regarded as sacred; wisdom was entrusted to the keeping of priest-philosophers; and they were permitted to communicate the choicest branches of the sciences only to duly initiated pupils. To bestow knowledge upon those who had not prepared their minds by years of discipline and self-purification profaned the mysteries, desecrated the sacred sciences.

Some years ago, in discussing this fine point in ethics with the late Professor James Breasted, the most distinguished of American Egyptologists, he confirmed my own findings; and further stated it to be his personal conviction that the classical civilizations concealed most of their learning under legends, myths, and allegories; and these have long been mistakenly accepted as the literal beliefs of these peoples.

There can be no doubt that the existence of a great continent in the Western Hemisphere was known to the ancient Greeks. And also to the Egyptians and the Chinese. It is nothing short of foolish to assume that the ancients lacked ships sufficiently seaworthy to navigate the larger oceans. Long before the Christian era, the older civilization had constructed boats far larger and more seaworthy than any of the vessels used by Columbus. One of the Ptolemys of Egypt built a ship large enough to have an orchard of fruit trees on the deck, together with swimming pools and fountains stocked with live fish.

Calculations based upon Plutarch's description of ancient voyages seem to indicate that the Greeks not only reached the coast of America, but explored the St. Lawrence river and part of the Great Lakes area. Plato, in his treatise on the destruction of Atlantis, wrote that due to the commotions in the ocean caused by the submergence of a vast continent, all navigation to the west ceased for a long period of time. This statement can only imply that such navigation had taken place in remote times.

Greek mythology perpetuates the knowledge of a blessed land beyond the Western Boundaries of Ocean. In this blessed land dwelt the Hesperides, the beautiful daughters of Night, and here also at the end of each day the sun came to rest. In popular mythology the Hesperic Isles were a kind of terrestrial paradise.

Thus, under a thin veil of mystic symbolism, was concealed the account of a Western continent of great size, fertile and rich and abounding in all good things.

The ancients believed the earth to be surrounded by the sphere of the constellations, and they assigned to each country the star groups which were above that country's particular area of land. In the arrangement preserved in the writings of Aratus of Soli, the constellation of the eagle spreads its wings accross the North American continent; the serpent winds its coil over Mexico and Central America; and the dragon floats in the sky above Japan and China. Perhaps Sir Edward Landseer was not far wrong when he declared that the symbols of nations, and the emblems pe-

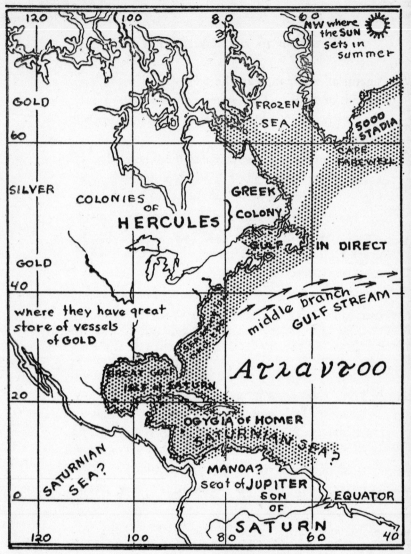

The existence of a great continent in the Western Hemisphere was known
to the ancient Greeks. This map presents in visual form Plutarch's description of ancient voyages for the guidance of navigators thirteen centuries before
Columbus. Distances by sea and the times and rates of travel are consistent

The narrative of Plutarch is substantiated by the Atlantic currents which the cautious ancient sailor followed as the natural route of travel, and he says of the latitude of the gulf which was the location of the Greek colony, it lies *"in a direct line over against that of the Caspian Sea"*

culiar to their heraldry, originated in their ruling constellations. Just about everyone knows that the constellation of the Great Bear is in the sky over Russia, and since time immemorial the bear that walks like a man has been the accepted symbol of the Russian State.

Thus in many ways we discover indications that the old races were wiser than we thought, and that what we have called discoveries are really only re-discoveries.

Beyond the western bounds of the ocean they located the fair land set aside by the gods to be the earthly paradise. Here in the fulness of time all men would come in search of the Golden Fleece which hung upon the tree sacred to the apples of the sun; and the early explorers did travel to the West in search of a Golden Fleece—the gold of the Incas, the treasures of the Aztecs, and the jeweled temples of the seven cities of Cibola.

It was in an old book which is in the British Museum that I found another and even more important key to the meaning of the Golden Fleece. It was known to the Greeks that the Golden Fleece was in reality a parchment on which was written the secret of human immortality. It was this parchment that Jason sought, for whoever discovered it would gain the secret of enduring empire, and power over the whole world.

We have now in America, enshrined in the Congressional Library, a Golden Fleece—the American Declaration of Independence, written on the skin of an animal and preserved as the magic formula of human hope. Those who understand it and can use wisely the import of its writings are possessed of the secret of the immortality of human society.

The curious fortunes of war brought another Golden Fleece from across the sea, and it is now preserved together with our own; this second parchment is the Magna Charta, the English bill of human rights which was the inspiration behind our American Declaration of Independence. These two immortal documents together form the declaration of the rights of man and are the basic texts of modern democracy.

By the wisdom then of those gods who are eternally vigilant over the needs of man, the blessed lands of the west were set apart, for none of the great civilizations of the past rose in North America to overshadow the continent with the ruins of old tradition, or to set up the corruptions of old administrative policy. Foreign nations came to this continent in times long ago; but they formed no permanent settlements nor attempted any program of colonization. And so the soil was not impoverished by thousands of years of intensive cultivation, nor were the natural resources ravished to supply the substance to maintain endless wars and ageless feuds.

It was the rise of the democratic dream in Europe that supplied the beginning of western civilization. Those in search of a promised land turned to the west. Here was a virgin continent populated only by nomadic Indian tribes, a vast territory suitable in every way for the great human experiment of the democratic commonwealth.

By the nineteenth century the American Hesperides was definitely the land of golden opportunity, and to it came streams of immigration from nearly every country on the earth. The better way of life drew them here, for it had been established that here men could build a future free of tyranny, intolerance, and enforced poverty. Here all were given opportunity for education, for free enterprise, and living a life according to the dictates of hope and conscience.

If in a comparatively short time many racial streams have met and mingled, and a new race has been born, the American race is not one to be determined by an analysis of blood or the proportions of the cranium. Americans are a race determined by the measure of a conviction, set apart by that conviction; it is the conviction that human beings are created free, and are entitled to equal opportunity to perfect themselves in life, liberty, and the pursuit of happiness.

And in recent years we have made another discovery. It is that the race of democracy is one distributed throughout the whole world. Among men and women of all races and all nations are those who share our conviction, and because they share it they are of our kind and belong to our race. In this realization we mark the beginning of world democracy.

Wise men, the ancients believed, were a separate race, and to be born into this race it was necessary to develop the mind to a state of enlightened intelligence. The old philosophers taught that physical birth is an accident, for men are born into various races and nationalities according to the laws of generation; but there is a second birth, which is not an accident; it is the consequence of a proper intent. By this second birth man is born by enlightened intelligence out of nation and out of race into an international nation and an international race. It is this larger and coming race that will some day inherit the earth. But unless a man be born again by enlightenment, he shall not be a part of the philosophic empire.

Our age of gold will pass and some day the Golden Age will come again. A future greatness is right now casting its long shadow across the face of Nature. With each passing generation the responsibilities of the American people will increase. More and more we shall be looked to as a source of courage, strength, and hope.

And it will be in this way that we shall fulfill the destiny for which our nation was created by dreamers of long ago. From the Blessed Isles of the West must come the fulfillment of the promise of the ages.

# 4

## THE FIRST ELECTION OF LAW-MAKERS

Solon, of Athens, freed the debtors' person to reform the institution of debt slavery; he instituted the selection of juries by lot, with all citizens participating; and he gave the voting franchise to all taxpayers alike, thus beginning national democracy six hundred years before Christ.... When he later journeyed to Egypt, he there learned of the first war of conquest, in the story of the lost Atlantis, and became acquainted with the imperishable laws for the government of nations.

When Solon, of Athens, visited Egypt he was taken by the priests to an underground river to view two columns on which were inscribed the laws given in olden times for the government of nations, not made by man but as the will of Eternal Nature

# 4

EBT has been the common
burden of the ages, and yet
the whole structure of our
modern economic world is
built on the shaky foundation of Bills Payable and
Bills Receivable. Long ago,
interest ate up its own
principal, and we are currently living on the interest on our own unliquidated debts.

Solon, greatest statesman of the Greek world,
was handed this age-old problem when, about
595 B. C., he was summoned to the leadership of
the State with the title, Archon. He was given
unlimited powers to reform the economic and
constitutional systems of the Athenians. His first
move was to attack the old Attic law of debt which
he believed lay at the source of the public dis-
tress.

In the time of Solon, the Greek countryside was
littered with roughly hewn stone markers. Origin-

ally these were boundary stones fixing the property lines of the lands of various citizens. As time had passed, it had become the custom to carve into these stones the records of mortgage contracts affecting the property which they bounded. Single stones became insufficient after a time, and eventually the added monuments to debt interfered with the plowing of the fields.

Solon, investigating the tragedy of the mortgage monument, made several interesting discoveries that were to change the course of human economics. When poor farmers mortgaged their lands to rich families on neighboring estates, and the debts were not paid, the wealthy landowners moved their boundary stones to include the encumbered property, and the previous proprietors became tenants. These tenants were obliged to pay one-sixth of their products for the privilege of working the soil; and if they failed their persons were attached and they became slaves. This was the Attic law which Solon abolished, the law which permitted loans on the security of the debtor's person.

When Solon restored the freedom of all who had been enslaved for debt, the reform was highly acceptable of course to the poorer classes; but it found little favor with the landowners. They im-

mediately set to work in a conspiracy to discredit
Solon and force him out of office. Thus, back in
very olden days, when life was very simple, the
basic problems which harassed the State and burdened the legislators stemmed from the persisting
fallacies of human nature.

In further effort to bring some semblance of
order out of the Athenian chaos, Solon also attempted a reorganization of social classes, giving
political existence to large groups never before represented in government. He divided the citizenry
into four groups reminiscent of old Brahman
castes. He then readjusted taxation so that the
poorer classes all paid equally an approximate 5
percent of their income. Equalizing the tax burden according to individual means paved the way
for an equality of representation in the governing
body. All citizens who paid taxes were entitled
to be heard in matters of the common good, and
were privileged to elect magistrates. These steps
marked the beginning of the democracy of the
ancient Greeks.

But the greatest of all of the reforms of Solon
took place in the courts of justice. Selection of
juries was by lot, with all citizens participating,
even the poorest; and these juries were upheld over
the pressures of established privileged groups.

One of the most curious of Solon's regulations throws light on the difficulties of his time. He forbade that a bride should bring to the house of her husband more than three changes of garment and 'like personal furniture.' He also ordained that each citizen must stand ready to show at any time to properly authorized persons how he obtained his living. Any citizen failing to do this would lose his franchise.

The drastic changes of Solon made him so many enemies that after a few years he felt he had to relinquish the burden of leadership of the State to regain his honor. Those who hated and feared him, as Archon, promptly renewed their love after he left public office and no longer threatened their ambitions.

His term as Archon brought to Solon the realization of his own inadequacy; and he visited Egypt in search of a larger wisdom. He was received with kindness and every mark of respect by the priests at Sais who served the shrine of the Goddess Isis. To these wise men he told the story of his effort to enlighten the Greeks, and correct the evils in their laws. The High Priest of Sais is reported to have said, "Alas, you Greeks, you are but children; for you know not the wisdom of the gods."

One night the priests of Sais led Solon through the long dark pasageways of the temple. They descended stone stairs rutted with age and lighted only by flaming torches, came at length to subterranean chambers hewn from the living rock. Through these chambers flowed a river. The priests said that this river was the sacred Nile that flowed from Egypt through the underworld to water the fields of the immortals. On the bank of the underground stream a small black boat was waiting, rowed by men who were blind.

Accompanied by the High Priest and the torch bearers, Solon was rowed out over the dark waters. The boat stopped on the shores of a tiny island far under ground. The light from the torches fell on two tall columns that glistened; they appeared to be made of some strange metal, covered with curious writing in an unknown language.

The High Priest, pointing his golden rod at the pillars, explained their mystery to the astonished Solon. These columns, he said, were placed on the island beneath the ground thousands of years ago by a lost people which had vanished forever from the earth. The pillars were of an unknown metal which neither rusted nor deteriorated with age.

He continued: Once long ago there existed on the earth a vast empire, the power of which extended to every corner of the world, and great fleets of merchant ships sailed the seven seas and brought their wealth to its fabulous city of the Golden Gate. Here there were schools for the study of the mysteries of Nature; towers for the examination of the stars; mines beneath the earth from which the precious metals were brought forth in abundance. This empire was ruled over by seven kings, who were the descendents of Neptune, God of the Seas.

Then came the fatal day when the seven kings of the Islands of the West in disobedience to the laws of the gods resolved to conquer the whole earth. And thus it was that war came into being, for before that time there had been no strife among men. And the seven kings led an army against the ancient Greeks and they invaded all of Europe, coming in great ships from the west. This, Solon was told, occured about 9000 years before the seige of Troy.

The gods were angry because the seven kings had made war. They caused the earth to be shaken and the great Islands of the West vanished into the sea. In a single night, sixty million human beings perished because they had disobeyed the laws of heaven. In time even the name of the Atlantic Empire was forgotten; for it must ever be so that those who disobey the gods shall vanish from the memory of mankind, regardless of their wealth or power.

"From these ancient columns" said the High Priest, "we have read the laws that were given in olden times for the government of nations. These laws are not made by men but are the will of Eternal Nature. Upon these laws enduring States must be built. To depart from these laws is to die. So perished the nations of the elder world."

When Solon returned to Greece it was his intention to take the story of the Atlantic Empire and develop it into a great epic poem; but the infirmity of years and the responsibilities of the State interfered. Instead, Solon told the story in the fullest detail to his close friend, Dropis, who in turn recited it to his son, Critias. In his 90th year, Critias communicated the narrative to his grandson of the same name who later became a disciple of Socrates. It is in this way that the story of the lost Atlantis came finally to be incorporated in the Platonic dialogues as part of a conversation between the younger Critias and his master Socrates.

The dialogue itself was named the *Critias*.

# 5

## THE ANCIENT LEAGUE OF NATIONS

A description of the lost Atlantis was written by Plato; it introduces the league formed by the ten benevolent kings who ruled over the lesser nations and the three great continents of Europe, Asia, and Africa; and who bound themselves by oath to obey the divine laws of enduring empire.... This was the philosophic democracy, with all men having the right to become wise through self-discipline and self-improvement, thus achieving the only aristocracy recognized by Natural Law.... The Atlantis story continues to the later decision of the kings to use their united power to enslave all the peoples of the earth, and the consequent destruction of Atlantis by earthquake and fire.... interpreted politically, it is the story of the breaking up of the ideal pattern of government.

 HE destruction of Atlantis, as described by Plato in the *Critias,* can be interpreted as a political fable. The tradition of the Lost Empire as descended from Solon was enlarged and embellished according to the formulas of the Orphic theology; but it does not follow necessarily that Plato intended to disparage the idea that a lost continent had actually existed west of Europe. Plato was a philosopher; he saw in the account of the fall of Atlantis an admirable opportunity to summarize his convictions concerning government and politics.

The *Critias* first describes the blessed state of the Atlantean people under the benevolent rulership of ten kings who were bound together in a league. These kings were monarchs over seven islands and three great continents. From the fable we can infer that the ten rulers of the Atlantic league were philosopher kings, endowed with all virtues and wise guardians of the public good. These kings obeyed the laws of the divine father of their house, Poseidon, god of the seas.

In the capital city of Atlantis stood the temple of Poseidon, and in it a golden figure of the god. In this shrine also stood a column of precious substance inscribed with the laws of enduring empire. The ten kings took their oath together to obey these laws, and they chose one of their number, usually of the family of Atlas, to be the chief of their league.

It was written on the column of the law that the ten kings of Atlantis should not take up arms against each other, for any reason. If one of them should break this law the other nine were to unite against him to preserve the peace.

In all matters concerning the public good the ten kings were to deliberate together, and each should be mindful of the just needs of the others; for they were the members of one body and regents over the lands of a blessed god.

The kings had not the power of life or death over any of their subjects except with the consent of the majority of the ten; and each was responsible to the whole league for his conduct in the administration of his own State.

In this way Plato describes the government of the Golden Age, in which men live on earth according to the laws of heaven.

By the three great continents of Atlantis are to be understood, Europe, Asia, and Africa; and by the seven islands, all the lesser peoples of the earth. The league of the ten kings is the cooperative commonwealth of mankind, the natural and proper form of human government. The Atlantis, therefore, is the archetype or the pattern of right government, which existed in ancient days but was destroyed by the selfishness and ignorance of men.

Plato, it must be remembered, was a monarchist by philosophic conviction, but his ideal king was the wise man perfect in the virtues and the natural ruler of those less informed than himself. This king was the father of his people, impersonal and unselfish, dedicated to the public good, a servant of both the gods and his fellow men. This king was descended of a divine race; that is, he belonged to the Order of the Illumined; for those who come to a state of wisdom then belong to the family of the heroes—perfected human beings.

Plato's monarchy was therefore a philosophic democracy; for all men had the right to become wise through self-discipline and self-improvement. One who achieved this state was by virtue of his own action a superior man, and this superiority was the only aristocracy recognized by Natural Law.

Competition is natural to the ignorant; and co-operation is natural to the wise. Obeying the pattern established by the gods, the divine kings bound themselves into the common league to obey its laws, preserve the peace, and punish any whose ambition might impel them to tyranny or conquest.

Here then, is a pattern of world government to insure the prosperity of all peoples and activate the preservation of the peace.

Plato describes at some length the prosperity of the Atlantic Isles under this benevolent rulership. The citizens were happy, and poverty was unknown. A world trade was established, and the ships of the Atlantean marine traveled the seven seas, bringing rich treasures to the motherland. There was little crime; the arts flourished; and the sciences were cultivated in great universities. Men had no enemies, and war was unknown.

The god Poseidon guarded the destinies of his domains and favored the Atlantic Empire with a good climate and fertile soil.

Men followed the occupations which they preferred and lived a communal existence, together sharing the fruits of their labors. It was Plato's conviction that the human being was not created merely to engage in barter and exchange, but rather to perfect himself as the noblest of the animals, endowed with reason and the natural ruler of the material world.

The *Critias* then describes the gradual change that came about in the course of the ages. In the beginning the Atlanteans saw clearly that their wealth and prosperity increased as a result of friendship. But gradually the divine portion of their consciousness began to fade away in them; their souls became diluted with a mortal admixture and human nature gained ascendency. They became unseemly and lost those spiritual virtues which were the fairest of their precious gifts.

It is the story of how man departed from the perfect pattern of his conduct, and in the end denied the very truths which were the foundations of his strength. With the loss of his spiritual perception, material ambitions increased, and the desire for conquest was born. Men yearned after that which they had not earned, and gazed with covetous eyes upon the goods of others.

The rulers of the State were corrupted by the common evil; the ten kings were no longer friends; they no longer conferred together in the temple of Poseidon to decide all matters under the common oath. Thus was the great league' dissolved by selfishness and ambition. It was then that war came into being, and with it tyranny and oppression, and despotism and the exploitation of peoples.

At last the kings of Atlantis decided to use their common power to enslave all the peoples of the earth. They gathered a vast army and attacked Europe from the sea, even going so far as to besiege the Athenian States. And so they broke the law of the gods; for the twelve deities had so divided the earth that to each race and nation was given its proper part.

Zeus, father of the gods, who carries in his hand the thunderbolts of divine retribution, perceived the evil of the time, and resolved to punish the arrogance of the Atlanteans. But even Olympus is a commonwealth, and the other eleven gods were summoned to the council hall of the immortals.

"When all the gods had assembled in conference, Zeus arose among them and addressed them thus—" ...it is with this line that Plato's story of Atlantis ends; and the words of Zeus remain unknown.

But the results of the conference are not left in doubt. Zeus hurled his thunderbolts against the empire of the sea, shaking it with earthquakes and then destroying it by horrible combustion. The only records that remained were in vague traditions and two columns set up under the temple at Sais.

The destruction of Atlantis can be interpreted politically as the breaking up of the ideal pattern of government.

So complete was this destruction, that men forgot there is a better way of life, and  since have accepted the evils of war and crime and poverty as inevitable.  The world lost too all sense of its own unity; each man's hand was thereafter raised against his neighbor.  The perfect state disappeared under a deluge of politics; the priests of Poseidon gave way to the priesthood of Mammon.

Plato's political vision was for the restoration of the Empire of the Golden Age.  The old ways of the gods must be restored, he was convinced, if human beings are to be preserved from the corruptions which they have brought upon themselves. Plato sought this end when he established his university at Athens—the first school of formal education in history.  Here men were taught the great truths of religion, philosophy, science, and politics, to restore to them the vision of the perfect State.

The old Atlantis was gone, dissolved in a sea of human doubts.  But the philosophic empire would come again, as a democracy of wise men.

Two thousand years later Lord Bacon re-stated this vision in his *New Atlantis*.

# 6

## A ROMAN PROJECT TO GIVE RULERSHIP
## TO THE WISE

The Platonic point of view was envisioned by Plotinus to
take form as a philosophers' city, establishment of which
was approved by his Roman emperor as the noblest experiment in time....But the fear of the Roman Senators
that the projected commonwealth of learning might finally
overthrow the empire brought the project to naught, as
Rome continued in the advanced state of smugness that
immediately preceded the complete collapse of the nation.

URING chess games played nearly seven hundred years after Plato's death, Plotinus, the greatest of the Neo-Platonists, discussed the problem of State with Galienus, Emperor of Rome. The Roman ruler was not a profound thinker, but he had an excellent mind which inclined toward the Platonic point of view, and he frequently sought advice from the great philosopher and mystic, Plotinus. This friendship led to Plotinus confiding to the emperor his dream of a philosophic city.

The situation and circumstances were impressive. One of the two men had the vision of the world's greatest need, the other had the power to make that vision a reality.

In the Compania, not far from Rome, stood the deserted ruins of an ancient city which had been destroyed by the vandalism of men and the crumbling forces of time; Plotinus asked that this become the site of a habitation for the learned, that here with funds raised from both public and private sources a noble community be built, to be ruled over by the laws set forth in the writings of Plato, and to honor the great man the city should be called Platonopolis.

Plotinus pointed out that such a project would not only bring honor to the wise but would confer immortality upon the name of the emperor, lasting dignity upon the whole of the Roman Empire. Galienus came to favor the project as the noblest experiment in time. But the Roman Senate viewed the matter with suspicion and alarm. To them it would be a serious misfortune for the aristocracy of wealth to be challenged by the aristocracy of learning!—the philosophers' city might finally overthrow the Empire. Always, philosophers had been especially troublesome to the smug, and Rome was in the advanced state of smugness that immediately preceded the complete collapse of the entire Empire.

So Galenius had to discover that emperors were not all-powerful; he was quietly informed by representatives of powerful and aristocratic families that if he continued to entertain seriously the dream of a philosopher's city it would be necessary to find as his successor a ruler with a more practical turn of mind. Plotinus and the emperor continued to play chess and conversationally build philosophic cities in the privacy of the royal apartments, and Rome continued on its headlong flight toward oblivion.

Excepting only recent years, this is the one time in history when a serious attempt was made to give wisdom a place in the temporal plan of living. Wise men are naturally endowed with the qualities of rulership, but they have had little if any voice in the rulership of the world; their voices have been heard only after the men themselves were dead. Plato lives thus today, and his words have a greater vitality in this century than they did in his time in ancient Athens.

An ever increasing thoughtfulness has resulted from the vicissitudes of recent years in bringing the realization that wars destroy not only the economic and political structures of nations, but the irreplaceable monuments of culture and learning which are the enduring wealth of empire. Great libraries are reduced to smoldering rubble by the engines of modern warfare, the art treasures of five thousand years vanish in the smoke of battle, and ruthless pillaging and wanton mutilation are the inevitable accompaniment of military aggressions. Both victor and vanquished are impoverished by a common loss, and posterity deprived of the noblest of its heritage.

This need not go on. The remedial action required is no more than for men to set aside in some selected part of the earth an area to be kept apart from all strife and struggle, and establish this as the common repository of the treasures of essential learning. On an island distant from strategic military objectives could be built a city of art, libraries, museums, universities, laboratories, and observatories. These institutions could be united as one great structure, a school over all schools, the city to become the capital of the intellectual empire. It might appropriately be named Platonopolis, to honor the great man who first conceived the idea of the commonwealth of learning.

In times of stress or danger each nation could send to this community those of its citizens whose mental excellence would entitle them to a world citizenship. Here, protected from all outside interference, they would be allowed to continue the various works of their individual lives for the enrichment of their own time and future ages, their progressed knowledge becoming the common property of all men, regardless of race or nation.

It is safe to predict that such a philosophers' city
would ultimately be the most practical and certain
instrument for accomplishing a world point of
view in all departments of human thinking. The
international nation—the dream of the future
which has been inspired by the terror of modern
warfare—would have its natural beginning in a
union of superior intellects.  Art knows no race;
music is a common denominator; biology and
physics are served by explorers into the furthermost
and innermost secrets of nature.  When we recognize that the poet, the scholar, and the savant are
indeed a race inhabiting the surburbs of a superior
world, that they are the noblest of our creatures,
we can know that we honor ourselves most by
honoring them.

Here lies the solution to the great educational
reform so necessary at this time.  We can not hope
to build a nobility of man upon the sterility of a
narrow, competitive, materialistic educational policy.  The ignorance of man has been his undoing.
Only wisdom can restore him to his divine estate.

The religious motion in the modern world is
away from theology and all the artificial limitations set up by creeds and dogmas.  To meet the

ever increasing dissatisfaction, there must be a new vision concerning the substance of spiritual truth. The religion of the future will include within its own structure the best of science, art, literature, politics, and sociology. Spirituality is not a blind faith about things invisible. It is an inspired use of things known and available. That man is religious who lives well. That man is sacrilegious who perverts universal good for purposes of private gain. The abstract parts of religion are useful only to the degree that they justify and prove the moral virtues.

From the broad gates of the philosophers' city could flow the inspiration for a completely new estimation of the Universe, and man's relationship to it. When the gentler parts of learning exercise dominion over the human mind, world peace will be more than the substance of things hoped for.

The Roman Senate now lies in its snug little tomb along the Appian Way. But unfortunately the temper of the Roman Senator still survives to oppose the unknown and defend private privilege against the world's necessity. And for this reason it may be as difficult to found the philosopher's city on the ruin of modern civilization as it was to build Platonopolis on the ruins of the old city of the Compania.

There is one difference, however. In the last 1800 years humanity has suffered its way a little nearer to a state of enlightenment. We are a little older and a little wiser than the Roman Senate. Education and science are lodged in institutions far stronger than in that day when wandering teachers held classes on doorsteps or along the country road. In every nation of the civilized world great institutions of learning have sprung up, richly endowed and fully equipped to meet the challenge of a new age. What these institutions lack is common spirit and common purpose, and an ideal strong enough to bind them into one great empire of learning.

When Plato dreamed of his wise man's world he set the chief place in it aside to be the temple of the Ever Living God. Here he proposed to set up once more the column of precious substance bearing upon it the laws of the immortals for the conduct of human affairs. To this shrine the learned would come again, to bind themselves with the great oath that they should dwell at peace each with the other, and serve all men, justly and without favor.

This oath is the beginning of learning and the end of strife.

# 7

## THE DEMOCRATIC TRADITION PRESERVED
## BY SECRET SOCIETIES

For more than three thousand years, secret societies have labored to create the background of knowledge necessary to the establishment of an enlightened democracy among the nations of the world....The Greek Dionysians were social and political temple builders, known as the Collegians in later Rome....The rise of the Christian Church brought persecution of the classical intellectual pattern's ideology, driving the guilds into greater secrecy; but all have continued searching for human happiness under a variety of rituals and symbols; and they still exist, as the Order of the Quest.

 ODAY'S thinking toward a democratic world state is neither a new trend nor an accidental circumstance; the work of setting up the background of knowledge necessary to the establishing of enlightened democracy among all nations has been carried on for many hundreds of years by secret societies.

Secret societies have existed among all peoples, savage and civilized, since the beginning of recorded history. The esoteric organizations of ancient times were for the most part religious and philosophical. In the medieval world they were philosophical and political. In the modern world, political and social.

Secret societies have had concealment and protection as the first purpose for their existence. The members of these orders were party to some special knowledge, they usually took part in certain rites and rituals not available to non-members, but it was more important that through the societies they were also able to practice beliefs and doctrines in private for which they would have been condemned and persecuted if these rites were made public.

A second purpose for secret societies was to create a mechanism for the perpetuation from generation to generation of policies, principles, or systems of learning, confined to a limited group of selected and initiated persons.

Primitive secret orders exist among African tribes, among the Eskimo, and throughout the East Indies and Northern Asia. The American Indian, the Chinese, Hindus, and Arabs have elaborate religious and fraternal organizations. In most cases these secret orders are benevolent and the members are bound together by obligations of mutual helpfulness and the service of the public good. It is beyond question that the secret societies of all ages have exercised a considerable degree of political influence, usually directed against despotism, intolerance, and religious fanaticism.

The Order of the Dionysian Artificers originated among the Greeks and Syrians at some remote

time before 1500 B. C.  It was composed originally
of skilled craftsmen, banded together in a guild to
perpetuate the secrets of their crafts.  Gradually
the science of architecture took precedence and
dominated the policies of the society.  According
to legend, when Solomon, King of Israel, resolved
to build his temple according to the will of his
father, David, he sent to Tyre and engaged the
services of a cunning workman, Hiram Abiff, a
master of the Dionysian Artificers.  The members
of this society held the exclusive right throughout
the Greek states of designing the temples of the
gods, the houses of government, the theaters of
Dionysius and the buildings used for the public
games.

It is certain that the Dionysians practiced secret
rites and worshipped the gods under geometric
symbolism; and that they possessed a body of lore
which included mathematical secrets of proportion
and design, certain knowledge concerning universal dynamics, and a philosophical, religious, moral
and political conviction concerning the perfecting
of human society.  They referred to ignorant and
uncultured humans as a rough ashlar, that is, an
uncut stone as it comes from the quarry, unsuited
to the purposes of building.  Through the refine-
ment which resulted from self-discipline and an

addiction to the divine arts, man perfected himself; becoming square, upright, and true, thus forming the true ashlar, or the cut stone which could fit with others into a pattern of masonry. In their secret work the Dionysians thus were social and political temple builders, and the temple upon which they labored was the living temple of the Living God, "built of stone made ready before it was brought thither; so that there was neither hammer nor axe nor any tool of iron heard in the house while it was in the building." This temple was human society perfected; and each enlightened and perfected human being was a true stone for its building.

As Grecian culture reached Rome, the Latins formed their own Dionysian soceity and named it the Collegia. The greatest of the Collegians was an architect, Vitruvius, sometimes called the father of modern architecture. A man of vast learning, he was responsible for the superior sanitation of Rome and the great aqueducts which still border the Appian Way. While the Collegia of the Romans was less philosophical than was the Grecian society, because of the different temper of the Latin people, it exercised considerable social power and perpetuated the substance of the old belief.

The rise of the Christian Church broke up the intellectual pattern of the classical pagan world. By persecution of this pattern's ideologies it drove the secret societies into greater secrecy; the pagan intellectuals then reclothed their original ideas in a garment of Christian phraseology, but bestowed the keys of the symbolism only upon those duly initiated and bound to secrecy by their vows.

Part of the Dionysian movement migrated eastward to build the empire of Islam with each stone in mosque and palace bearing the mark of the master masons. Later the migration continued as far as India, where these same marks are to be seen on the monuments of the Mogul dynasty.

In early development of Europe the Dionysians became the guild of the cathedral builders. They signed each stone with the secret symbols of their cult, and into the intricate carvings of church and chapel they worked the old pagan figures and designs. Many guilds sprang up, binding skilled craftsmen in confraternities of arts and crafts and trades. Architecture remained the chosen instrument for the perpetuation of the Great Design— the building of the perfect world.

All the sciences contained brilliant far-seeing men who equally desired to contribute their part to the philosophic empire of the future. Secret societies were formed in their own professions, using the emblems established in their arts to conceal their social aspirations. Thus did the Alchemists come into being, the mystic chemists seeking the elixir of life, the wise man's stone, the universal medicine, and the agent for the transmutation of metals.

The elixir of life is truth itself, the preserver of all things.

The wise man's stone is science, that can work all wonders and solve all riddles of the mortal sphere.

The universal medicine is wisdom, the only cure for ignorance, which is the universal disease.

The agent for the transmutation of metals is the pattern of the Universal State, the essence of the perfect plan for a world civilization by which all the base elements in human society can be transmuted into the spiritual gold of right purpose.

In Italy, the Illuminati sought for the pearl of great price hidden in the deep waters of mortal corruption.

In northern Europe, the Knights of the Holy Grail dedicated their lives to the search for the chalice of the passion.

Christian and Jewish cabalists pondered the letters of the scriptures to find the secret of the crown of splendors, and the Rosicrucians in their hidden houses used the Rose of Sharon as the symbol of brotherly love, a simple rearrangement of the letters r-o-s-e becoming e-r-o-s, the Greek God of love, Eros.

All these groups belong to what is called The Order of the Quest. All were serching for one and the same thing under a variety of rituals and symbols. That one thing was a perfected social order, Plato's commonwealth, the government of the philosopher-king. To this end each consecrated its life and knowledge, exploring ever further into the secrets of Nature to discover the greatest secret of all—the secret of human happiness.

We are indebted to these Brothers of the Quest for our sciences, arts, and crafts of today. They were the discoverers; they were the astronomers, scientists, physicians, mathematicians, and artists whose works we treasure but whose dreams we have ignored. They gave knowledge to the world to make men happy. We have used their knowledge to make a few men rich. We have perverted their skill, desecrated their dreams, and profaned their mysticism. But the knowledge they have given us is available to be used in a nobler way, and some day we shall awaken to our responsibility with the realization that it is our common duty to restore the dignity of learning and dedicate it unselfishly to the human need.

About the middle of the 17th Century, Sir Elias Ashmole, patron of the liberal arts and founder of the Ashmolian Museum at Oxford, was initiated into the guild of the operative freemasons of London, the first non-craftsman to be permitted membership. From that time on, the entire pattern of the guilds was changed, and speculative masonry came to dominate the older form of the craft, and the intellect builder came into his own. One veil of the old symbolism was lifted, to reveal in full clarity that the guilds were dedicated to a program social and politcal.

In this way the old dream of the philosophic empire descended from the ancient world to modern time. Secret societies still exist, and regardless of the intemperance of the times, they will continue to flourish until the Quest is complete.

For more than three thousand years, secret societies have labored to create the background of knowledge necessary to the establishment of an enlightened democracy among the nations of the world.

# 8

## A NEW IDENTITY FOR CHRISTOPHER COLUMBUS

Many scholars were fully aware of the global form of the earth in the time of Columbus, who, according to early historians, State documents, and his own son, was not an Italian of humble station and uneducated but was a Greek Prince with an excellent classical education....It was from a Greek port that he sailed on the celebrated voyage of discovery. He was accompanied by a mysterious stranger, which has suggested that Columbus was an agent of the society of unknown philosophers....The pattern of the democratic ideal was beginning to assert itself over the tyranny of decadent aristocracy. A new world was necessary for a new idea....When it was necessary, it was discovered.

*NOTE: The University of Barcelona has pronounced genuine a document discovered by an Italian archeologist in 1929. It records that the treasurer of Spain counseled Colon to represent himself as Christophorens in demanding aid from the King of Spain, and states emphatically that Admiral Colon was not the same man as Christophoro Colombo, son of Dominico and Susana Fontanarossa who lived in Genoa.*

The cipher signature of Columbus (reproduced above) is generally interpreted *Salve Christus, Maria, Yosephus-Christoferens.* It was usual to build personal ciphers upon dates. If the seven large letters above the signature are read according to the medieval system of numeration the date 1420 results. The "x" appears to be a double letter composed of "jx"; this would increase the sum to 1430. Is this then the true and unknown birthdate of the *Greek* navigator?

S stated earlier, there can be little doubt that the Greeks were aware of the existence of the American continent long before the beginning of the Christian era. If information is not general on that point, it is equally surprising how little is known about the man Christopher Columbus who is acredited with the discovery of the new world. The date of his birth is unrecorded, and twenty cities claim Columbus as a native. So many legends have sprung up about this strange man that it is difficult to distinguish fact from fancy.

In 1937 a little book was published, entitled, *Christopher Columbus Was A Greek*. According to its author, Spyros Cateras, the real name of Columbus was Prince Nikolaos Ypsilantis, and he came from the Greek Island of Chios. The statement is backed by quotations from numerous early historians and State documents.

The author of this little book has documented his opinions in a manner to bring joy to the critical reader. He mentions the following Greeks who navigated the Atlantic ocean in ancient times: Hercules, Odyssus, Colaeus, Pytheus, and Eratosthenes. He points out that the language of the ancient Mayas of the American continent contains many words of pure Greek belonging to the Homeric period, and, to quote the book: " Years ago, in the republic of Uruguay, South America, were discovered traces of the army of Alexander the Great, swords and thoras with the inscription 'PTOLEMEOS ALEXANDROY'!".

All modern research on the life of Columbus tends to prove that he was not a man of humble station, poor or uneducated, and the story of Queen Isabella and her jewels is rapidly becoming recognizable as fiction. Columbus is emerging as a man of impressive personality with marked abilities as a leader and organizer and an excellent classical education.

Like most Greeks of his time he admired the writings of Plato and the other classical philosophers; he had the Greek birthright of legend and tradition, and was mentally well suited for interpretation of classical lore. There is much to indicate that Columbus was inspired for his voyages by Plato's account of the lost Atlantis and the records of early navigation to the West. Furthermore, Europe was not without some knowledge of geography and in his day there were many scholars aware of the spherical form of the earth.

A great trade with Asia had long passed over the caravan routes of the Near East, as the Arabs for the most part were a friendly people; but with the rise of the Turkish Empire to power most of these routes were closed to the infidel. When even the Crusades failed to keep clear the roads of commerce, it became ever more desirable to discover a western passage to the Orient. It was for this purpose that Columbus sailed, and not from an Italian or Spanish port, but from the Greek port of Mahon.

It is astonishing how difficult it is to ascertain the facts about the celebrated voyage of discovery and the life of one so prominent in history as Christopher Columbus; it appears that history entered into a conspiracy to conceal the truth. Possibly an elaborate misrepresentation was intentional, for certainly the confusion began before the death of Columbus. His own son refers to his father as a Greek. It has been suggested that Columbus changed his name because of religious or political pressure, but this is in the field of conjecture.

Then too, in browsing about among old records I have run across a dim figure involved in the life of Columbus, a strange man who seems to have served the explorer in the capacity of counselor. Nothing very tangible has as yet come to light, but it is hinted that this mysterious person accompanied Columbus on his first voyage. He was not included in the list of the mariners. He did not return, but remained in the West Indies; beyond this, no further mention is made of him.

This mysterious stranger is reminiscent of the black-robed man who guided the destiny of Mohammed. Were these obscure figures ambassadors of the secret government?—Columbus being one of the agents through which the society of unknown philosophers accomplished its purposes?

It is my opinion that he was such an agent. The signature of Columbus, composed of letters curiously arranged and combined with cabalistic designs, certainly conveys far more than is inherent in the signature of a private citizen.

The importance of Columbus in the larger scheme of things is to be estimated from his relationship to the pattern of his own time. Europe, passing from the obscuration of the medieval period, was coming into the light of the modern way of life; the motion of the Rennaissance had spread like ever widening ripples over the surface of a stagnant pool. Printing had been discovered; the mental emancipation of man from the tyranny of ignorance, superstition, and fear was gradually being accomplished. The democratic ideal was beginning to assert itself over the tyranny of decadent aristocracy.

As the mental horizon broadened, the physical horizon extended also. The Crusades had broken up the structure of feudalism. Principalities were forming themselves into nations, and the tribal consciousness was disappearing from the theater of European politics. This progress was opposed at each step by vested interests. But the human mind was becoming aware of its own powers, in a motion of continuing irresistible force.

A new world was necessary for a new idea. When it was necessary it was discovered. That which is needed is always near if man has the wit to find it.

Today we are again seeking for a new world. No longer do there remain undiscovered continents to serve us as laboratories for social experiments, so we are turning our attention to other kinds of worlds—worlds of thought, inner spheres which must yet be explored by daring navigators. Science in the last fifty years has discovered a new universe—the universe of the mind. The infant psychology has but to come of age for us to fully discover a new sphere for new exploration in the science of living.

The voyages of Columbus were followed by two centuries of enlarging our geographic knowledge of the earth. Explorers who sailed the seven seas seeking wealth, brought home knowledge; it released human thought from its Mediterranean fixation and accomplished the still greater end of breaking the power of a Mediterranean theology and a Mediterranean way of life. Men began to think world thoughts, began to realize that while the whole earth was one land divided into continents and oceans it still was a gigantic unity. Out of the global wanderings of stout sea captains in little wooden ships was developed our so-called global thinking of today.

The concept of a global world, at least in terms of geography, is now our common inheritance. After four hundred and fifty years we accept it without question, but mainly to toy with the belief that we will accomplish something in terms of ultimates if we can industrialize the entire planet. Our world is still too large for us to know how to use it. We have discovered much, but the greatest voyage still lies before us.

Our venture will be into that greater ocean that lies beyond the boundaries of the known. The new voyages will be made in laboratories, and the contrary currents will be the cosmic rays that move through the seas of universal ether.

This will require of each man that he make a long journey of discovery within himself, searching out the hidden places of his mind and heart. As Socrates so wisely observed, all mankind lives along the shore of an unknown land. This unexplored world abounds in wonders and is filled with riches beyond the wildest dreams of old Spanish conquistadores. In this land beyond the sea of doubt the wise men dwell together in shaded groves, and here, according to the old tradition, the scholar, the musician, the artist, and the poet —who makes the discoveries that science and philosophy must later prove—have already found the better way of life.

Christopher Columbus sailed his little ships for a land which by the writings of ancient philosophers he knew existed. And each of us in the fulness of time will make our own voyage in search of a philosophically-charted better world—to follow the advice of Homer, to prepare our ships, unfurl our sails, and facing the unknown go forth upon the sea to find our own far distant native land.

# 9

## THE PROPHECIES OF NOSTRADAMUS

Eleven years after Columbus reached our shores, an extraordinary man was born in France. In adult life he was
both a respected physician and a mystic who was able to
write accurately the history of the world to come....
There was no indication at the time that in the Western
Hemisphere would arise a great nation, but Dr. Michel
Nostradamus saw a civilization established there that
would observe (always on a Thursday) a day to express
thanksgiving for freedom of religion, freedom of opportunity, and freedom of life....He prophesied that this
nation would free itself from the bonds of the mother
country, would greatly prosper, but would have to fight
several wars—one with the Orient—before becoming a
great power in a pattern of world peace, with other nations looking to it for leadership....All that he foretold
is precisely according to the Platonic tradition.

ISTORIES are generally written about the men who prominently influence the events that make history; little is written—though it might be of greater interest—about those shadowy figures who seem always to stand behind the men who make history.

Michel Nostradamus, seer of France, is among the most extraordinary of such men; born in 1503, and possessed of some inner source of knowledge beyond the reach of ordinary mortals, he wrote the history of the world to come!

Two hundred years later, the celebrated Illuminist and Rosicrucian, the Comte de St. Germain, remarked to his close friend, Prince Carl of Hess-Cassel, that he was the one who had assisted Nostradamus in the calculation of his remarkable predictions.

91

All this is far too shadowy for sober historians, although a number have spent considerable time and developed numerous headaches trying to trace the life of the illusive Comte, who was called by Frederick the Great, "The man who does not die."

Nostradamus was a respected physician, a man of outstanding medical accomplishments. Few details of his life are available, but from the context of his manuscripts, his epistles to the King of France, and his letters to his own son, it is evident that he too belonged to the Order of the Quest. Mystic, philosopher, astrologer, alchemist, and cabalist, Nostradamus was versed in all the secret lore disclosed only to those who have bound themselves with the oath of the brotherhood.

The prophecies of Nostradamus might have come entirely as revelations of the spirit; but it is equally possible that in his quaint old doggerel verses he included part of the plan of things to come as already well set in the minds and purposes of his brother initiates.

The first edition of the *Prophecies of Nostradamus* was published in 1660. At that time the Americas were still the happy hunting ground of Spanish adventurers. There was no indication that in the Western Hemisphere would arise a great nation. Yet Nostradamus writes at sufficient length of the future state of America to indicate an extraordinary knowledge.

The old seer refers to this country under several names. He calls it the Hisparides, the Blessed Isles of the West. In another place he simply names it America. And his third designation of it is, the Land Which Keeps the Thursday.

This last form is the most astonishing. For it refers to the unique American holiday, Thanksgiving, which always falls upon a Thursday. And this the only holiday which depends upon the day alone for its observance, and is peculiarly the American holiday which expresses thankfulness for freedom of religion, freedom of opportunity, and freedom of life.

To summarize the opinions of Nostradamus concerning the future destiny of Western civilization is difficult, because of the involved idiom of the original text. But he points out clearly certain things that will happen. He saw that a great civilization would rise in the western world. This civilization would free itself from the bonds to its mother country, and then assume a free place among the temporal powers. The new country would flourish and extend its domain across the entire continent. It would grow rich and powerful, he predicted, and live at peace with its sister,

(Canada). He said that America would have to fight several wars, including one with the Orient. This conflict he describes as an eagle flying against the rising sun, and in his day neither the eagle nor the rising sun had significance of the slightest importance in the symbolism of nations.

Fulfilling its destiny, Nostradamus foretold that America would become a great power in a pattern of world peace and would be looked up to by other nations for leadership against the common evils of the time. In short, as Nostradamus foretells the story of the Blessed Isles it is precisely according to the Platonic tradition; and we can not but wonder if he was a party to that tradition, and knew exactly whereof he spoke.

Whether the 16th Century physician of France had his visions from within himself, or whether he merely wrote down what was given to him by another, we can never know. Conventional thinkers, doubting such prophetic powers, incline toward the second alternative. And that will leave them scarcely less comfortable of mind, for the existence of this secret brotherhood plan is then virtually admitted.

Nostradamus is not the only prophet who sensed or knew the future of western empire. There was Dr. Ebenezar Sibly, who flourished in

England about the close of the 18th Century. It is reported that Sibly had a shrewish wife and it was to escape her tongue that he retired to a garret of his house to ponder the mysteries of the Universe, his meals being passed to him through a hole in the door. Dr. Sibly divided his time between an infallible elixir which, if dissolved in wine, would dissolve all human ills, and the writing of long books dealing with astrology, physiology, and anatomy.

In his day, the American republic was in its infancy; and brilliant politicians on the floor of the House of Commons were predicting that the rebellious colonies would soon be begging on bended knee to be restored to the British commonwealth. Sibly, though a stout Britisher, expressed his regrets that he had to point out that, in one detail at least, an astrologer in his garret would prove wiser than the best politicians in Europe, for sad to relate, the American colonies would not come home—the stars decreed otherwise. Not only would they remain outside the fold, he said, but they would grow rich and powerful; extending themselves across their continent, Americans would build great cities and develop world trade and industry. And, one day—horrible thought!—they would be stronger than the mother country! And this was the truth that must be spoken, if only through a hole in a garret door.

It should be remembered that among the ancients, astrology was one of the sciences of government. The prognostic aspect of the subject was not the main interest in the minds of such men as Pythagoras and Plato; these philosophers saw in the motion of the heavenly bodies and the order of the cosmos a great pattern of natural laws. The Universe was a celestial empire populated with planets, and suns, and moons, in a heavenly arrangement which was a clue to the proper distribution of human affairs. The State, they advocated, should be patterned after the Cosmos. Governments of men should be in harmony with the larger government of the world.

Many old astrological books indicate clearly that planetary symbols were used to represent the elements of a political system, and that the astrologers themselves were part of the Order of the Quest. Beneath the cloak of professional astrologers, they were counselors advising kings and princes to establish better laws and rule their peoples more wisely.

Nostradamus was consulted by three kings. Europe's most powerful Queen, Catherine de Medici, also consulted him on numerous occasions.

His advice was always temperate and directed toward the public good. His scholarship gave a perspective on political problems that was beyond the scope of the professions of statescraft.

All the petty princes of Europe in medieval times had their Merlins, wise old men who in many instances were the actual rulers of the State. It is obvious that if these counselors were bound together by some common purpose their collective power would be considerable. And they were bound together, in the secret society of unknown philosophers, moving the crowns of Europe as on a mighty chess board. Men of this calibre bring about the mutations of empire. It is the general opinion that revolutions begin with the common people, but this is not true; the benevolently informed always guide and direct public opinion.

Through the centuries the prophesies of Nostradamus have continued to exercise a powerful force on the political destiny of the world. They have been translated into most of the languages of Europe; they were frequently quoted and reprinted during the period of the First World War; and in the Second World War both the Axis and the Allied powers have quoted Nostradamus variously to serve their purposes.

It is in the larger picture of the world's future that Nostradamus indicates the coming of the great league, or assembly of world powers. This league is to be the only human hope of peace, the only solution to a competition between nations. The formation of this league begins the new life of the human race, will allow the human being at last to emerge into the estate for which he was fashioned.

Barbarism ends with the beginning of world civilization. To be civilized, according to Cicero, is to reach that state of personal and collective behavior in which men can live together harmoniously and constructively, united for the betterment of all. By this definition, we have never been civilized. We have existed in a state of cultured savagery.

The promise of Nostradamus is especially meaningful in these difficult years; for he assures us that the commonwealth of nations is to become a reality.

# 10

## THE DESIGN OF UTOPIAS

Sir Thomas More wrote a fable, about four hundred years ago, to set forth the social state of man in a philosophic commonwealth, but so completely has the world missed the entire point, that the very word "Utopia" is even today a synonym for optimistic but impractical ideals of reform....Campenella, an Italian philosopher, wrote of the major tragedy in that the subject of statesmanship alone had been neglected as practically every other subject had been reduced to a science. Government officials, he insisted, should be elected after examination to determine knowledge and fitness....Boccalini contributed further to Utopian literature, and Andreae sought to Christianize it, with the theme: "For lack of vision the people perish."

The men who through the centuries have envisioned
Utopia belong to ages yet unborn, when the principles of
natural philosophy will be applied to the problems of
government and social dilemmas will be examined for
solutions which are now termed impractical

NE of the best known and least read of the world's literary productions is Sir Thomas More's *Utopia*. It was composed by a man who had suffered greatly from the political corruption of his day, 1478-1535; having held high office, More was well acquainted with those machinations commonly called conspiracies of the State.

More should properly be regarded as a Platonist, too; for the entire framework for the *Utopia* is borrowed from Plato's *Republic*, and the book is permeated throughout with Platonic ideology concerning the ideal State. Under a thinly veiled satire attacking the policies of King Henry VIII, here then is another voice calling men to the correction of their political vices.

Unfortunately, the immediate success of More's book was due to his attack on the King and the government in general, rather than any serious considerations of the remedies which he suggested.

In the *Utopia,* More presents his philosophical and political conviction in the form of a fable which sets forth the social state of man in a philosophic commonwealth. So completely has the world missed the entire point that More attempted to emphasize, that the very word "Utopia" has become a synonym for optimistic but impractical ideals of reform.

Sir Thomas More was centuries in advance of his day, which was reason enough why he could not be appreciated. Together with the master, Plato, More belongs to ages yet unborn, to the time when men weary of study of the dilemmas which now they examine by what they think is practical, will turn to solutions which they now term impractical.

An important Utopian was Tommaso Campenella, 1568-1639, an Italian philosopher also with strong Platonic leanings. Out of the wisdom of his years, Campenella composed the *Civitas Solis,* the city of the sun. In this work he departed from his usual interests—science, mathematics, and religion—to apply the principles of natural philosophy to the problems of government. He regarded it as a major tragedy that men had reduced to a science practically every branch of learning except statesmanship, which continued to be left to the vagaries of incompetent politicians skilled only in the arts of avarice.

Unfortunately, Campenella was not able to free his mind entirely from the pattern of his contemporary world, so his ideals are confused and not entirely consistent. He viewed government as a kind of necessary evil to be endured until each man shall become self-governing in his own right. To the degree that the individual is incapable of the practice of the moral virtues, he must be subjected to the laws which protect him from himself. and protect others from his unwise actions. The principal purpose of life then is to release oneself from the domination of government by the perfection of personal character.

Campenella envisioned the perfect State as a kind of communistic commonwealth in which men shared all the properties of the State, receiving more or less according to the merit of each one's action. His theory that the State should control propagation is a little difficult in application, but his advice that all men should receive military training as part of their education would meet present favor. Government officials, he insisted, should be elected by an examination to determine knowledge and fitness, and promotion should be by merit alone and without political interference.

This view is definitely Platonic, and leads naturally to Plato's conception of the philosopher-king as the proper ruler over his people.

Campenella may have intended his *City of the Sun* to be a philosophic vision of a proper world government, or may have been setting forth no more than the basis for a new constitution for the City of Naples, which at that time was looking forward to the estate of a free city. It is also said of Campenella that he lacked the beauty and idealism of the greater Platonists, and while this is probably true, his book is witness to the ills of his own time and a reminder to us that most of the evils he pointed out remain uncorrected.

In the year 1613, Trajano Boccalini, aged seventy-seven, was strangled to death in his bed by hired assassins. At least this is one account. We are informed by another historian that he died of colic. A third describes his demise as a result of being slugged with sand bags. Anyhow, he died. And it is believed that Trajano's end was due to a book which he published entitled, *Ragguagli di Parnaso,* a witty exposition of the foibles of his time.

The 77th section of this book is titled, "A General Reformation of the World." Like the other

Utopians, Boccalini made use of a fable to point out political evils and their corrections: Apollo, the god of light and truth, is dismayed by the increasing number of suicides occurring among men. So he appoints a committee composed of the wisest philosophers of all time to examine into the state of the human race. These men bring a detailed account and numerous recommendations to Apollo. Nearly every evil of modern government is included, ranging from protective tariffs to usury in private debt. The final conclusion reached by the committee is that the human problem is unsolvable except through a long process involving suffering and disaster. As an immediate remedy the best that could be done was to regulate the price of cabbages—which seemed to be the only article not defended by an adequate force of public opinion or a large enough lobby in places of power.

Boccalini's satire is important because it constituted the first published statement of the Society of the Rosicrucians. It points out that, first, evils must be recognized; then, the public must be educated to assume its proper responsibility in the correction of these evils; and lastly, public opinion must force the reformation of the State and curb the ambitions of politicians. This was a solemn pronouncement in the opening years of the 17th

Century. It is little wonder that it cost Boccalini his life.

Johann Valentin Andreae, an early 17th Century German Lutheran theologian, was the next to cast his lot with the Utopians. Andreae's status is difficult to define, but he is generally believed to be at least the editor of the great Rosicrucian *Manifestos,* and the author of the *Chemical Marriage of Christian Rosencreutz.* We may therefore safely assume that he was connected with one of the great orders of the Quest.

Andreae's contribution to the Utopian literature is his *Christianopolis,* or the City of Christ. This work, which is almost unknown to English readers, is largely developed from the ideas of Plotinus. *Christianopolis* is Platonopolis, Christianized. Its author was a quiet scholar with a long white beard and a strict sense of Lutheran propriety. His *Christianopolis* is a monument of morality and good taste, but beneath his strict orthodoxy, Andreae was a man of broad vision. His city is governed by the wise and is enriched with all the arts and sciences; there is no poverty. The citizens are happy because each is performing his task motivated by an understanding of the dignity of human life.

To my mind, it is dignity of values that makes *Christianopolis* a great book. In order to live wisely, men must have a sense of participation in the present good and future good. There must be a reason for living. There must be a purpose understandable to all, vital enough and noble enough to be the object of a common consecration. Andreae tells us again and again, in the quaint wording of his old book, "For lack of vision the people perish."

It remained for the master of all fable, Sir Francis Bacon, to bind together the vision of the Utopias with supreme artistry. It is a philosophical catastrophe that Bacon's *New Atlantis* was left unfinished. Or *was* it left unfinished? Rumor has it that the book was actually completed but was never published in full form because it told too much. The final sections of Bacon's fable are said to have revealed the entire pattern of the secret societies which had been working for thousands of years to achieve the ideal commonwealth in the political world.

I have examined two old manuscripts relating to this subject and found them most provocative; but it might be less to the point to discuss that which Lord Bacon was compelled to conceal, when there is so much that is worthy of our consideration in the parts of the work actually published.

# 11

## THE OBJECTIVE OF THE SECRET
## SOCIETY

One reference to a secret society in Bacon's *New Atlantis* is scarcely less than a proclamation of the Society of Unknown Philosophers, but has gone unnoticed for three hundred years....This fable is of the land of Bensalem, meaning the Son of Peace, which with its merchandise, the Light of Truth, maintained a trade with Atlantis, which was declared to be the same as America....Every thing indicates that it was Sir Francis Bacon's dream that the enlarging of the bounds of human empire should be instituted on our own continent, an area peculiarly set aside by Nature for the perfection of philosophy and the sciences.

HE writings of Sir Francis Bacon are generally grouped under three headings—professional, literary, and philosophical. Each of these groups contains a variety of important works. But Lord Bacon's mind, taste, and conviction are best revealed through his philosophical writings. In this group are works that are strictly philosophical, others that verge toward the sciences, and still others which sum up convictions relating to all branches of knowledge.

Possibly the most remarkable of Lord Bacon's ethical contributions is the fragment called the *New Atlantis,* which forms a kind of gloss upon his principal philosophical production, the *Instauratio Magna.* To Bacon, the greater part of learning was the application of knowledge to the necessities of the human state. It was only natural that he should envision the results should his inductive system be given Universal application.

The *New Atlantis* was first published in 1627, as a kind of appendix to the *Sylva Sylvarum,* a natural history in ten centuries. On the title page is a curious design. It shows the figure of an ancient creature representing Time drawing a female figure from a dark cavern. The meaning is obvious: Through time, the hidden truth shall be revealed. This figure is one of the most famous of the seals or symbols of the Order of the Quest. Contained within it is the whole promise of the resurrection of man, and the restitution of the divine theology.

The *New Atlantis* was not published during the recorded lifetime of Lord Bacon. It was issued the year following his death by His Lordship's chaplain, William Rawley. This man was Bacon's close friend and familiar over a period of many years, and most of Bacon's papers were entrusted to Rawley's care. In his admiration for Bacon's personal character and philosophical powers he left the expressed wish to be buried at his master's feet, and his wish was fulfilled.

Rawley writes in his introduction to Bacon's the *New Atlantis,* "This fable My Lord devised, to the end that he might exhibit therein, a model or description of a college, instituted for the interpreting of nature, and the producing of great and marvelous works, for the benefit of men; under the name of Solomon's house, or the college of the six days work."

The college of the six days work is, of course, a thinly veiled reference to the perfection of nature through art. The six days are the days of creation by which the natural world was brought into existence, according to the account given in Genesis. As God created the Universe in six symbolic days, so man by art—that is, philosophy—must create the condition of his own perfection by means of six philosophical steps.

The college is the secret school—the wise man's 'house' wherein are taught all arts and sciences, and not according to a materialistic interpretation, but according to a divine understanding of causes.

Rawley stated that it had been His Lordship's intention to complete the fable of the *New Atlantis* with a second part, to contain the laws of the Ideal State, or commonwealth of the wise. Since it was Bacon's custom to prepare numerous drafts of his writings in the process of perfecting them, it is probable that the second part existed at least in outline; but Rawley would not have felt it proper to publish the part which His Lordship had not perfected in literary form.

It is well known among the secret societies of Europe that the second part of the *New Atlantis* exists. It includes a description of a great room in Solomon's house wherein are displayed the crests and the coats of arms of the governors of the philosophic empire. It may be for this reason that the writings were suppressed, for these crests and arms belonged to real persons who might have been subjected to persecution, as Sir Walter Raleigh was, if their association with the secret order had been openly announced.

The fable of the *New Atlantis* begins with a ship sailing from Peru for China and Japan being driven from its course by contrary winds. Those aboard after many months faced death by starvation and disease. They prayed to God for help, and their prayer was answered; the ship came at last to the fair harbor of a great city in an unknown land. Here the mariners were hospitably received and after certain formalities were permitted to land; and the wonders of the city were then revealed to them.

The title page of Bacon's masterpiece, *Novum Organum,* features a small sailing ship between two columns. These columns are the pillars of

Hercules, the Strait of Gibraltar, which marked
the western boundary of the sea. The little ship
is science, sailing forth from the limits and boundaries of the old world into the unknown sea of
Universal learning. Is not this the same ship that
finally came to haven in the Wise Man's City?

The *New Atlantis* describes the magnificence of
the college of the six days work. Here the wise
dwelt together in a gentle commonwealth of learning. One of the wise men makes the following
statement in a prayer:

"Lord God of Heaven and Earth; Thou hast
vouchsafed of Thy grace to those of our *Order,* to
know Thy works of creation, and the secrets of
them; and to discern (as far as appertaineth to the
generations of men) between divine miracles,
works of nature, works of art, and impostures and
illusions of all sorts."

It is difficult to understand how this reference
to a secret order has passed unnoticed for so long,
for it is scarcely less than a proclamation of the
Society of Unknown Philosophers.

The name of the land in which stood the Wise
Man's City was Bensalem; this means the Son of
Peace. Bensalem maintained a trade with all parts
of the world, but not for gold, silver, jewels, silks,
spices, nor any other material commodity; its

merchandise was the Light of Truth. Among the nations traded with was Atlantis, which was declared to be the same as America.

The college of Solomon's house had ambassadors, agents, and representatives among all the nations of the world, so that all discoveries in the arts and sciences might be known to it. In great libraries all useful records were stored up for the service of future ages.

The book closes with a long lecture delivered by one of the Fathers of Solomon's house. This great dignitary summarized the work of the brotherhood in the following magnificent statement— one which might well be inscribed over the doors of learning and in the hearts of all scholars, scientists, and philosophers:

"The end of our foundation is the knowledge of causes, and secret motions of things; and the enlarging of the bounds of human empire, to the effecting of all things possible."

The Father of the wise men then described the laboratories, observatories, mines and hospitals; and the various engines and inventions by which the elements could be controlled and the secrets of Nature discovered. There were gardens for the study of plants, and parks filled with birds and animals so that men could investigate their habits.

Even reptiles, insects, and fishes were considered and their uses classified.

Medicines of all kinds were distilled and compounded, and mechanical arts were perfected according to the laws of Nature.

There were houses where the senses of man were studied with the aid of perfumes, flavors, sounds, music, and extraordinary accoustical devices.

And there were houses where only deceits were on record, so that the methods by which men can be deceived could be made known and studied.

In the philosophical city all men were employed according to their tastes and ability, and each contributed in his own way to the sum of useful knowledge. There were museums where rare and excellent inventions were preserved, and galleries containing the statues of great men who had contributed to the improvement of the human race. Among the statues was one to Christopher Columbus; another to the man who had invented bread.

The narration ends abruptly with the word of the editor that the rest was not perfected.

Missing is that part which was to describe the laws of a philosophical commonwealth. It is safe to assume that these laws, like the whole pattern of the story, were the same set forth by Plato for the government of the wise.

Everything indicates that it was Bacon's dream that the college of the six days should be erected in America, an area peculiarly set aside by Nature for the perfection of philosophy and the sciences.

Part of this dream has been realized. In this land are the greatest laboratories, observatories, and institutions of research that the world has ever known. We are exploring into the mysteries of the atoms and the electrons, and have brought the heavenly fire, electricity, to be the servant of our purposes.

All that remains is to crown science with philosophy. As we perfect the inner part of learning the philosophic empire will arise in human society.

# 12

## WESTERN CULTURE A THOUSAND YEARS
## BEFORE COLUMBUS

In the Mexican area the civilization then existing was the most advanced on the earth....The ancient Mayas had massive public buildings and observatories in at least a hundred cities, and these were connected by broad paved highways. Rulers were elected by the common agreement of the people. The Mayas hold the world record for a continued peace of five hundred years; this has been attributed to their having possessed no monetary symbol or currency for goods exchange. Theirs was the first democratic State on a continent set aside for the perfection of the dream of democracy....Long before the coming of the white man, the spirit of human equality, human cooperation, and freedom of worship had flourished here.

As today's archeologists continuously study the massive ruins of the Mayan civilization we know that this ancient culture of the American continent included at least a hundred cities connected by an intricate pattern of broad paved highways. Their language was suited to the expression of exact knowledge

I N the jungles of Yucatan, Guatemala, and Honduras are the ruined cities of a lost civilization which flourished on the North American continent a thousand years before the voyage of Columbus.

Stuart Chase has made the observation that in the five centuries immediately following the beginning of the Christian era, the civilization of the Mayas was the most advanced existing on the earth.

Very little is known of the Mayas, their origin, history, religion or culture, because of the wholesale destruction of Mayan writings and historical records in the early years of the Spanish conquest. Massive ruins of their buildings remain, and great stone tablets; but these are in a language as yet undeciphered. From the physical evidence and the material remains we know that the empire of the

Mayas extended over a very large area; included were at least a hundred cities, connected by an intricate pattern of broad paved highways. Enough of the art of the Mayas has survived to entitle them to a high place in the sphere of creative aesthetics; and their massive stone and plaster buildings prove that they possessed a well developed knowledge of architectonics. They had observatories for the study of the arts and developed a highly accurate calendar. Their written language, more complicated than the Chinese, is of a type suited to the expression of exact knowledge and the most refined mental and emotional reflexes.

According to their own legends the Mayas owed their cultural superiority to a mysterious old man who came out of the sea riding on a raft of serpents. Among various tribes this man has different names, but he is best known by the title conferred upon him in the Mexican area. Here he was called Quetzalcoatl. He is said to have come from the east from the land of the many colored rocks. Quetzalcoatl carried with him the symbol of the cross. His name means the "feathered snake," or the "serpent covered with the plumes of the Quetzal bird."

The Feathered Snake taught the people of Central America all of the useful arts and raised them from a primitive state to one of an excellent civilization. He instructed them in agriculture, architecture, medicine, science, language, religion, and statesmanship. Having accomplished the civilization of the Indian tribes, he ruled over them for a time as a benevolent priest-king. Then he returned to the shore of the sea, called to his raft of serpents, and then floated away to the east, with the promise to return at a distant day to rule over his nation.

When Cortez reached the coast of Mexico the Aztec King, Montezuma, dispatched messengers of State bearing with them the plumed crown of Mexico. The trusting Aztec thought that Cortez was Quetzalcoatl returned, and was ready immediately to surrender the throne!

The Mayan Empire was the highest civilization to be developed in the Americas. Also, it was the first great democratic State on a continent curiously set aside for the perfection of the dream of democracy.

So far as we know, the rulers of the Mayas were not hereditary, but were elected for life by the common agreement of the people. They seemed to have governed wisely and to have fulfilled the classical requirements of priest-kings. The priesthood itself was powerful but benevolent, given to learning, and a patron of the arts and sciences. The religion consisted of a monotheism, that is, the worship of one Supreme Principle abiding in the sun.

Next to Deity, peculiar veneration was given to the Feathered Snake, who was regarded as a kind of Messiah, who suffered, died, and arose again. The legend of Quetzalcoatl was thus in parallel with the myth of the dying God, very much as in Egypt, Chaldea, Greece, and as expressed by the early Christian Church.

The Mayas were not a warlike people, and there is no support for popular belief that they were by nature cruel or barbaric. On the altars of their gods they offered only flowers and fruit; and it was not until the decline of the empire and its domination by less advanced tribes that human sacrifice was practiced, and then only on the rarest occasions.

It is believed that the Mayas hold the world record for continued peace. They flourished as a great powerful nation for five hundred years without war with other tribes or internal strife.

The high civilization attained by the Mayas was due primarily to the laws given them by Quetzalcoatl. So long as they obeyed these laws they continued to prosper. Unfortunately we have no complete record of their legal codes, but we do know a few of the outstanding principles which lay at the root of their State.

The Mayan nation was a collective commonwealth living under an advanced form of socialized order. They possessed all goods in common, and shared equally in the benefits of their production. They possessed no money or monetary symbol of any kind; and it has been suggested that this lack of currency was in part responsible for their five hundred years of peace.

To them the wheel was the symbol of death, and they never developed any form of mechanized industry. Each gave a part of his goods to maintain the State, and this contribution was employed to build public buildings, parks, schools, and places of public sport.

There seems to have been no poverty, and little if any crime. No buildings have been found which suggest prisons or other places of confinement.

The Mayas were hospitable, kindly, gentle, and industrious; their cities were beautiful in every way; they were public spirited, well governed, and according to the order of their time, highly educated.

The religious temper of the people can be gathered from remnants that still survive. It is common to all the Indians of the Americas that religious intolerance is utterly beyond their comprehension. They look upon each man's religion as his own particular belief, and if it suits his needs it deserves the respect of all other right-minded men.

Thus we see that the archetype for a generous and enlightened way of life is part of the American continent's common inheritance.

It is well to note in passing that many of the simpler virtues practiced by the Mayas were shared by other tribes that inhabited North and South America. Although the North American Indians never achieved the high culture reached by the Mayas, all lived according to a democratic tradition. The members of all tribes took care of their aged, provided for the widowed and the fatherless, and severely punished in the rare instances when some tribesman attempted to exploit another. Tribal government was invested in a council of the older and the wiser, and all matters relating to the common good were submitted to them for arbitration and solution. Crime was almost unknown.

As most tribes were nomadic they had little opportunity to develop inter-tribal points of view, and so there was considerable strife between tribes, but even in their warfare, North American Indians respected valor and developed chivalry to a marked degree.

The first League of Nations was created among the Great Lakes Indians of the American North-east. First, five tribes, and later seven, combined under the leadership of the brilliant Indian leader, Great Rabbit, whose life has descended to us in Longfellow's poem, *Hiawatha*. The league of the seven nations was originally intended to be defensive, but also useful in settling inter-tribal disputes. It resulted from the simple discovery by aboriginal minds that one lived longer, more safely, and more happily if disputes among peoples were solved by arbitration rather than by open strife.

The Incas of Peru are second to the Mayas in the building of empire in America. Inca communities were also cooperative, and many of these villages still survive in the distant and less accessible high lands of the Andes. These were the only civilized communities in our land that never learned that there was a world depression beginning in 1929.

Rooted in the American continent is a long and distinguished tradition that points toward ability for leadership in the postwar world, along lines of cooperation and the international point of view.

The democracy established by thirteen colonies in 1776 was not the first American democracy. At least two thousand years before the coming of the white man, the spirit of human equality, human cooperation, and freedom of worship flourished here.

# 13

## BACON'S SECRET SOCIETY IS SET UP
## IN AMERICA

Men bound by a secret oath to labor in the cause of
world democracy decided that in the American colonies
they would plant the roots of a new way of life. Brotherhoods were established to meet secretly, and they quietly
and industriously conditioned America to its destiny for
leadership in a free world. ...Benjamin Franklin exercised
an enormous psychological influence in Colonial politics
as the appointed spokesman of the unknown philosophers;
he did not make laws, but his words became law.

OLONIZATION of the Western Hemisphere was largely motivated in the desire to pillage the fabulous treasures of the new world. The explorers, led on by legends of hoards of gold and silver, and palaces encrusted with jewels, formed expeditions often financed from their own purses but sometimes subsidized by the State. The Spanish were the most successful in their quest for riches; the majority of the other adventurers profited little and suffered much; and it soon became apparent that only by sober colonization was any sizeable reward to be gained in the new world.

For the promulgation of the Christian faith, the Western Hemisphere offered virgin territory. With the Conquistadores came priests, eager to convert

127

pagan tribes and nations to the faith of the old world. A holy inquisition was set up in New Spain, and Indians by the tens of thousands were tortured and killed for the good of their immortal souls. It was due to the zeal of the priests that the libraries of the Mayans were burned and their historical records destroyed.

To this day there stands in Merida, on the peninsula of Yucatan, the house of the Conquistador Montejo. Over the door of this house are the heraldic arms of this Spanish adventurer. The shield and crest are upheld by Spanish soldiers standing on the heads of tortured and enslaved Mayan Indians.

Reasonably accurate accounts of the natural advantages and resources of the Americas were in time brought back by the explorers and adventurers who had opened the new territories of the West, and only then did the European nations give serious consideration to actual development of their newly acquired colonial empires. The French, the Dutch, and the English entered upon programs of establishing permanent settlements along the Atlantic seaboard. The English program was under the direction of Sir Francis Bacon, and it was his genius that gave purpose to the enterprise.

Bacon quickly realized that here in the new world was the proper environment for the accomplishment of his great dream, the establishment of the philosophic empire. It must be remembered that Bacon did not play a lone hand; he was the head of a secret society including in its membership the most brilliant intellectuals of his day. All these men were bound together by a common oath to labor in the cause of a world democracy. Bacon's society of the unknown philosophers included men of high rank and broad influence. Together with Bacon, they devised the colonization scheme.

Word was passed about through secret channels that here in the Western Hemisphere was the promised land of the future. Here men of right purpose could build a new way of life, free from the religious intolerance and political despotism that held Europe in its clutches.

The history books tell us that the colonists made the long and dangerous journey in small ships in order to find a place where they could worship God, each according to the dictates of his own conscience. There is however much more to the story than our historians have dared to suggest.

Among the colonizers were some who belonged to the Order of the Quest, but it was not long before religious strife broke out in the colonies, for men do not change their natures merely by changing their place of habitation. Much of the intoler-

ance of the old world came over to plague the beginnings of the new civilization. It was not easy
to preserve high principles in pioneering a country.
A lot had to be done before the philosophic empire
could emerge out of the simple struggle for existence. And much has yet to be accomplished; we
are still pioneering in the sphere of right thinking
and right living.

Bacon's secret society was set up in America before the middle of the 17th Century. Bacon himself had given up all hope of bringing his dream
to fruition in his own country, and he concen-
trated his attention upon rooting it in the new
world. He made sure that the American colonists
were thoroughly indoctrinated with the principles
of religious tolerance, political democracy, and social equality. Through carefully appointed representatives, the machinery of democracy was set up
at least a hundred years before the period of the
Revolutionary War.

Bacon's secret society membership was not
limited to England; it was most powerful in Ger-
many, in France, and in the Netherlands, and most
of the leaders of European thought were involved
in the vast pattern of his purpose. The mystic
empire of the wise had no national boundaries and
its citizenry was made up of men of good purpose

in every land.  The Alchemists, Cabalists, Mystics, and Rosicrucians were the incisive instruments of Bacon's plan.  Representatives of these groups migrated to the colonies at an early date and set up their organization in suitable places.

One example will indicate the trend.  About 1690, the German Pietist theologian, Magistar Johannes Kelpius, sailed for America with a group of followers all of whom practiced mystical and esoteric rites.  The Pietists settled in Pennsylvania and their descendents still flourish in Lancaster county.  Kelpius for some years lived as an Anchorite in a cave located in what is now Fairmount Park, Philadelphia.  The Pietists brought with them the writings of the German mystic, Jacob Boehme, books on magic, astrology, alchemy, and the cabala.  They had curious manuscripts illuminated with strange designs, and their principal text was called *"An A B C Book for Young Students Studying in the College of the Holy Ghost."*  The Pietists brought the order of the Mustard Seed, and the Order of the Woman in the Wilderness to the new world.

Kelpius was a man of feeble health and after a few years died from the hardships and exposures of his religious austerity.  The inner circle of his order was composed entirely of celibates, and as these died there were none to take their places; and so far as the public knows, his secret society did not survive. Actually it did continue; but with the changing of the times it returned again to its secret foundations, disappearing entirely from the public view.

The early years of the 18th Century brought with them many changes in the social and political life of the American colonies. By this time most of the Atlantic seaboard was dominated by the English. Cities had sprung up, important trade flourished with the mother country, and the colonial atmosphere was in small counterpart that of the English countryside.

By this time most of the important secret societies of Europe were well represented in this country.

The brotherhoods met in their rooms over inns and similar public buildings, practicing their ancient rituals exactly according to the fashion in Europe and England. These American organizations were branches under European sovereignty, with the members in the two hemispheres bound together with the strongest bonds of sympathy and understanding. The program that Bacon had outlined was working out according to schedule. Quietly and industriously, America was being conditioned for its destniy—leadership in a free world.

Any account of secret societies in America would have to include tribute to the man who has been called the "First American Gentleman"—Benjamin Franklin. Although Dr. Franklin was never the country's President, nor a military general, he stands out as one of the most important figures in the struggle for American independence. Quiet, dignified, scholarly and gentle, Franklin foresaw a new goal for an ever changing world through the square bi-focal glasses of which he was the inventor.

Historians have never ceased to wonder at the enormous psychological influence which Franklin exercised in colonial politics. But up to the present day, few indeed are those who have realized that the source of his power lay in the secret societies to which he belonged and of which he was the appointed spokesman. Franklin was not a law maker, but his words became law. Beneath the homely wisdom which he circulated in his Almanac, under the pseudonym of Poor Richard, was a profundity of scientific and philosophic learning. He understood both the farmer and the philosopher, and could speak the languages of both.

When Benjamin Franklin went to France to be honored by the State, he was received too by the Lodge of Perfection, the most famous of all the

French secret orders; and his name, written in his own fine hand, is in their record ledger, close to that of the Marquis de Lafayette.

Franklin spoke for the Order of the Quest, and most of the men who worked with him in the early days of the American Revolution were also members. The plan was working out, the New Atlantis was coming into being, in accordance with the program laid down by Francis Bacon a hundred and fifty years earlier.

The rise of American democracy was necessary to a world program. At the appointed hour, the freedom of man was publicly declared.

# 14

## A PROPHECY WRITTEN IN THE YEAR OF WASHINGTON'S BIRTH

Sir William Hope noted the birth overseas of an infant starred by fate to rule both freemen and slaves, and named the year of the American Declaration of Independence forty-four years before it was signed. He gave in Cabalistic form the patriot leader's name, and the years of his lifetime span. ...The prophecy also singled out Abraham Lincoln, designated the term of Benjamin Harrison as the one to mark the first century of the new nation's progress....It is a reasonable assumption that the Hope prophecy is a genuine example of fore-knowledge of the destiny of the United States.

George Washington had just been born when the governor of Edinburg Castle wrote a prophecy that this infant born overseas was starred by fate to lead the colonies to freedom; this prediction also named, four decades in advance, the year of the Declaration of Independence

N the Congressional Library at Washington, D. C., is a curious little book entitled, *Vindication of the True Art of Self Defense.* It is a work on fencing and dueling, published in 1724 by Sir William Hope, Bart., a deputy governor of Edinburg Castle. In this copy and facing the title page an engraving has been inserted of the badge of the Royal Society of Swordsmen; underneath it is written, "Private Library of Sir William Hope." The Library of Congress has had this book since 1879.

The text of this curious little book is of no special interest, but on the blank flyleaves is written in the hand of Sir William Hope an extraordinary prediction concerning the destiny of the United States of America. It was written, signed and dated forty-four years before the beginning of the Revolutionary War.

At the time the thirteen American colonies sem-ingly had no dream of independence. George Washington had just been born, in Virginia. Twenty of the fifty-six men who were to sign the Declaration of Independence were then small boys, and eighteen others were yet unborn.

Little information is available concerning Sir William Hope; but from the text of his prediction it appears that he was devoted to the study of astrology, and based his strange prophetic poem upon an interpretation of the starry influences. There is also a hint of the Cabala in the manner used by Hope to indicate the men referred to in his prediction.

The prophecy of Sir William Hope begins with these lines:

> 'Tis Chaldee says his fate is great
> Whose stars do bear him fortunate.
> Of thy near fate, Amerika,
> I read in stars a prophecy:
>
> Fourteen divided, twelve the same,
> Sixteen in halfs—each holds a name;
> Four, eight, seven, six—added ten—
> The life line's mark of Four gt. men.

From the text, the prophecy covers the period from 1732 to 1901. From the history of our country during this period of time, Hope selected four men, and the numbers which he used to indicate them are shown as the prophecy unfolds. He summarizes the lives of these four men by totaling the number of years that each lived. He does this in the line, *Four, eight, seven, six—added ten—"* Four plus eight, plus seven, plus six, equal 25, the added ten is the cipher making a total of 250. At the time of his death George Washington was 68, Abraham Lincoln 56, Benjamin Harrison 68, and William McKinley 58. The total of these years is 250.

The next twelve lines are devoted to a description of George Washington and the struggle of the American colonies for independence.

> This day is cradled, far beyond the sea,
> One starred by fate to rule both
>     bond and free.

The prophecy is dated 1732, and in that year George Washington was born beyond the sea, in Virginia. The reference to bond and free is believed to indicate that slavery would exist during Washington's time in the colony of Virginia.

> Add double four, thus fix the destined day
> When servile knees unbend 'neath
>     freedom's sway.

By double four we can read 44, which if added to the date, 1732, gives 1776, the year of the American Declaration of Independence.

> Place six 'fore ten, then read the patriot's
> name
> Whose deeds shall link him to a deathless
> fame.
> Add double four, thus fix the destined day

There are six letters in the name George, and ten in Washington, and this Cabala when added to the previous and subsequent descriptions, can leave no doubt as to the man intended in the prophecy.

> Whose growing love and ceaseless trust
> wrong none
> And catch truth's colors from its glowing sun!
> Death's door shall clang while yet his
> century waits,
> His planets point the way to other's pending
> fates.

These lines contain not only a glowing tribute but an exact bit of prophesy. Washington died on December 14, 1799, just 17 days before his century passed into history.

Till all the names on freedom's scroll shall fade,
Two tombs be built, his lofty cenotaph be made—

Freedom's scroll is the Declaration of Independence, which is now carefully preserved under yellow cellophane because the signatures have begun to fade. The body of George Washington has rested in two tombs; and his lofty cenotaph, the Washington Monument, is 555 feet high, the tallest memorial ever constructed to the memory of a man.

Full six times ten the years must
onward glide,
Nature their potent help, a constant,
prudent guide.

If six times ten years, or sixty years, be added to the date of the death of Washington the result is 1859, when John Brown raided Harper's Ferry and was hanged for attempting to incite a slave revolt, a circumstance leading directly to the United States of America engaging in the great Civil War to preserve the freedom of all of its people.

Then fateful seven 'fore seven shall sign
heroic son
Whom Mars and Jupiter strike down
before his work is done.

When cruel fate shall pierce, though
    artless of its sword;
Who leaves life's gloomy stage
    without one farewell word.
A softly beaming star, half veiled
    by Mars' red cloud
Virtue, his noblest cloak, shall form
    a fitting shroud.

There are seven letters in Abraham, and seven letters in Lincoln. He is the "heroic son" elected to the Presidency in 1860, re-elected in 1864, and assassinated April 14, 1865. He was indeed struck down before his work was done, for slavery was not abolished by constitutional amendment until the end of that year, and the Civil War was not proclaimed to be at an end until August 20, 1866.

The reference to life's gloomy stage is the more extraordinary because Lincoln was assassinated at Ford's Theater while watching a play; and he never spoke again after the assassin's bullet struck him although he lived for several hours.

References to President Benjamin Harrison are contained in the two following lines:

Then eight 'fore eight a later generation rules,
With light undimmed and shed in progress'
    school.

There are eight letters in Benjamin, and eight in Harrison. He ruled in a later generation, 1889 to 1893. His administration was justly climaxed by the great Columbian Exposition at Chicago in 1893. Here, invention, transportation, industry, art, science, and agriculture exhibited the progress which they had made in the first century of American national existence. This is probably the 'progress school' referred to in the prediction. Harrison's administration was not dimmed by war or by any scandals in high office.

> Then six again, with added six shall rise,
> Resplendent ruler—good, and great—
>     and wise.
> Four sixes hold a glittering star that on
>     his way shall shine;
> And twice four sixes mark his years
>     from birth to manhood's prime.

While the verses accurately describe President McKinley, this is the only instance in which the numbers do not appear to fit the name. Research, however, indicates that the original form of the family name would permit it to be divided, thus, Will-Mc Kinley, which means, Will, the son of Kinley. In this form, each of the combinations

would contain six letters. Four sixes, or 24, agrees
with President McKinley being the 24th man to
hold the presidential office. And twice four sixes,
or 48, was the age of McKinley at the time he was
elected Governor of his native state, which might
be said to be his 'manhood's prime'. There is no
reference to McKinley's second term or his assas-
sination. But the prophecy definitely states that it
goes no farther than the end of the 19th Century.
It does indicate earlier however, that McKinley's
life was to be 58 years, which was correct.

The prophecy ends with four more lines:

> These truths prophetic shall completion see
> Ere time's deep grave receives the
>     Nineteenth Century!
> All planets, stars, twelve signs and
>     horoscope
> Attest these certain truths foretold
>     by William Hope.

Following this, is the statement that the prophecy was 'Writ at Cornhill, London, 1732.' At
the bottom of the page are four other lines written
by some later member of the Hope family as a
tribute to the memory of Sir William Hope:

> The learned hand that writ these lines
>     no more shall pen for me,

Photographic facsimile of the prophecy of Sir
William Hope, from a book which has been in
the Library of Congress for more than 60 years

Yet voice shall speak and pulses beat
    for long posterity.
This soul refined through love of kind
    bewailed life's labors spent,
Then found this truth, his search from youth,
    Greatness is God's accident.—

                James Hope

As is usual with material of this kind, efforts have been made to prove the Hope Prophecy to be a forgery; but up to the present time no tangible evidence has been advanced to disprove the prediction. Always in these matters, the critic takes the attitude that such predictions can not be made, and if a writing appears to be authentic then it must be imposture. The book has been in the Library of Congress for more than 60 years. The prediction about both Harrison and McKinley relate to incidents taking place after the book was placed in the Congressional Library.

In facsimile, one of the two pages of the original prophecy is illustrated here; both have every appearance of being genuine and authentic.

It is most reasonable to assume that the Hope prophecy is a genuine example of foreknowledge concerning the future of the United States of America.

# 15

## THE UNKNOWN MAN WHO DESIGNED
## OUR FLAG

Our flag was worked out in elements of design that provided for gradual modification in the future as the national destiny increased. It was a learned stranger, added by seeming accident to the committee appointed by the Colonial Congress in 1775, who had the foresight to provide the area for the stars in subsequent substitution for the British Union Jack. The design was adopted by General Washington; there is no record that the committee ever made a report to Congress....According to the rules laid down by Francis Bacon for works published under the authority of the society of unknown philosophers, each book must be so marked as to be readily recognizable. The book that tells of the presence of the unknown designer ends with a quotation from Bacon.

OBERT Allen Campbell in 1890 published a little book *Our Flag, or The Evolution of the Stars and Stripes.* Diligent research fails to uncover any data about Mr. Campbell. He states in his preface that the work is "a compilation of facts and dates from official sources, larger works, occasional pamphlets and addresses upon this and collateral subjects; and is meant, therefore, for the perusal of those who have not the time, opportunity or disposition for a more extended study in this line of research."

Then he refers specifically to the chapter of interest to our present consideration: "That part of this sketch which treats of the proceedings of the Congressional Committee in relation to the Colonial Flag, and of the unofficial consideration, by a

147

few of our Revolutionary statesmen and heroes, in regard to the Flag of the 'Thirteen United States,' immediately preceding its adoption by Congress, has not heretofore been published."

This last statement makes it extremely difficult to trace Mr. Campbell's source of information. We are forced to the conclusion that the story must have been given to him by word of mouth.

The book itself must have been printed in a very small edition, for it has become exceedingly scarce and is seldom if ever offered for sale. On those rare occasions when copies have changed hands, the book commands a price far in excess of usual works in this field.

According to the rules laid down by Sir Francis Bacon for works published under the authority of the society of unknown philosophers, each book must be marked in some peculiar way, easily recognizable by the informed, but not conspicuous to those who are not a party to the plan. All of the older writings are so marked, either with ciphers, curious headpieces, vignettes, colophons, designs, symbols, figures, or signatures. It is possible that the book, *Our Flag* carries such a signature; for it ends with the following quotation, "Out of monuments, names, words, proverbs, private records and evidences, fragments of stories, passages

in books, and the like, we save and recover some-
what from the deluge of time."—Bacon.

One thing is certain, Robert Allen Campbell has
concluded his treatise with a curiously meaningful
passage from the writings of the man responsible
for the broad program of colonization in the western world that made possible the creation of the
United States of America. The selection of Bacon's words to conclude the book may be accident,
and it may be intent; but in the light of the text
and the air of mystery which covers the history of
the writing and the life of the author, it appears
more than possible that intent is the answer.

Chapter 2 of *Our Flag* is entitled, "The Colonial
Flag" This in substance is what it says:

In the fall of 1775, the Colonial Congress in session at Philadelphia appointed Messers. Franklin,
Lynch, and Harrison as a committee to consider
and recommend a design for a Colonial Flag. General Washington was then in camp at Cambridge,
Massachusetts, and the Committee went there to
consult with him.

While at Cambridge the committee men were
entertained by a patriotic and well-to-do citizen.
At that time the best room in this gentleman's
residence was temporarily occupied by a peculiar
old gentleman. As there was only one other guest

room, Messrs. Lynch and Harrison were given the unoccupied room, and Dr. Franklin shared apartments with the old gentleman.

Nothing is known about the mysterious old man except that he was referred to as the "Professor"; his name is not preserved. He was beyond seventy years of age but apparently in the prime of his life. He ate no flesh, fish, nor fowl, or any green things, and drank no liquor, wine, or ale. His diet consisted of cereals, well ripened fruit, nuts, tea, and such sweets as honey and molasses. He was well educated, highly cultured, of extensive as well as varied information, and very studious. He spent most of his time pondering over rare books and ancient manuscripts, which he seemed to be deciphering, translating, or rewriting. These he kept carefully locked up in a heavy iron-bound chest and never showed them to any person.

He was liberal but in no ways lavish with his money, but was well supplied with all that he needed.

The Professor was a staunch advocate of democracy and his favorite statement was, "We demand no more than our just due; we will accept and be satisfied with nothing less than we demand."

On the eve of their arrival, December 13, the committee men dined with their host and hostess, also General Washington and the Professor. The Professor was introduced to the visitors without his name being given, and his ease, grace, and dignity during the introduction is especially noted. When Benjamin Franklin was presented, he stepped forward and extended his hand, which the Professor heartily accepted. As their eyes met there was an instantaneous, a very apparent, and a mutually gratified recognition.

After dinner, Washington and the committee men exchanged a few words in undertone, and then Dr. Franklin arose, saying, in substance, "As the Chairman of this committee, speaking for my associates, and with their consent, and with the approval of General Washington, I respectfully invite the Professor to meet with the committee as one of its members; and we, each one, personally and urgently, request him to accept the responsibility, and to give us, and the American Colonies, the benefit of his presence and his counsel."

After graciously accepting the invitation, the Professor made his first recommendation. He pointed out that the Committee now consisted of six persons, General Washington and the host being honorary members. Six was not an auspicious number, and as none of the members could be spared, let the hostess be included so that the number could be increased to seven. This suggestion was unanimously accepted and the hostess became the secretary of the committee.

The committee met the following evening in the Professor's room. General Washington opened the proceedings by asking Dr. Franklin for his recommendations. Franklin replied by requesting that the entire committee listen to the words of his new found and abundantly honored friend, the Professor, who had definite suggestions to make.

After a preamble, the Professor made the following extraordinary remarks:

"The sun of our political air, like the sun in the heavens, is very low in the horizon—just now approaching the winter solstice, which it will reach very soon. But, as the sun rises from his grave in Capricorn, mounts toward his resurrection in Aries, and passes onward and upward to his glorious culmination in Cancer, so will our political sun rise and continue to increase in power, in light, and in glory; and the exalted sun of summer will not have gained his full strength of heat and power in the starry Lion until our Colonial Sun will be, in its glorious exaltation, demanding a place in the governmental firmaments alongside of, coordinate with, and in no wise subordinate to, any other sun of any other nation upon earth."

The Professor went on to point out that the flag which he recommended would be subject to change in the future as the national destiny increased. This change, however, should not require a complete re-designing but a process of gradual modification: "To make it announce and represent the new nation which is already gestating in the womb of time; and which will come to birth—and that not prematurely, but fully developed and ready for the change into independent life—before the sun in its next summer's strength ripens our next harvest."

The design finally submitted consisted of a field of thirteen alternate red and white stripes, and in the area which now contains the stars was the British Union Jack. The area containing the Union Jack was the one suitable for modification. The design was formally and unanimously accepted, and the flag was adopted by General Washington as the recognized standard of the Colonial Army and Navy. There is no record of any report being made by this committee to Congress.

On January 2, 1776, at Cambridge, in the presence of the Army, General Washington with his own hands raised the newly made flag on a tall and specially prepared pine tree liberty pole. The British army at Charleston Heights could see the flag clearly. After inspecting it with their field glasses, the British officers ordered a salute of thirteen cheers, followed by a regular official salute of thirteen guns in honor of the new standard. It appears therefore, that the Colonial Flag was as pleasing to the British as it was to the Colonies.

It is easy to see why Mr. Campbell's story has received very little recorded recognition. It belongs among those shadowy and mysterious happenings which influence or change the course of empire but will ever find little favor with prosaic and unimaginative historians.

# 16

## THOMAS PAINE AND THE RIGHTS
## OF MAN

The crusading of Tom Paine definitely advanced for Americans that secret destiny by which all people shall be free and equal. There is little doubt that he assisted Jefferson in writing the Declaration of Independence.... Paine emphasized the necessity of separating the spheres of Church and State in government, preached religious tolerance in a day when the spirit of persecution was still strong, attacked the special privileges of the aristocracy... Only by thousands of years of conditioning can mankind be brought to the perfectionist state envisioned by this American patriot.

Of Thomas Paine it has been said that he did more to
win the independence of the colonies with his pen than
George Washington accomplished with his sword. Only
complete reorganization of government, religion, and education would bring us even today to the perfectionist state
Tom Paine envisioned

# 16

HE stormy petrel of Revolutionary days in America and France was Thomas Paine. Son of a hard working Quaker who made his living cutting barrel staves, young Thomas's formal education ended in grammar school; he practiced his father's trade for a time before turning his mind to politics and the social problems of his time.

Benjamin Franklin inspired Thomas Paine to become a champion of human rights. Their first meeting took place in England, and at Franklin's suggestion Paine came to America and entered into the publishing business. English born, he became an outstanding champion in the cause of freedom for the colonies. His writings so fanned the flame of patriotism that it has been said of him that he did more to win the independence of the

157

colonies with his pen than George Washington accomplished with his sword.

There is little doubt that Thomas Paine assisted Jefferson in writing the Declaration of Independence. Present research even points to the probability that he composed the entire document, then submitted it to Jefferson for editing and revision. The references in the Declaration of Independence to "the Laws of Nature" and "Nature's God" especially reflect Paine's theological convictions.

Paine held several offices in the Continental government during the period of the Revolutionary War, and in 1789 returned to Europe. Three years later he published his *Rights of Man*. Although the truths contained in the essay were never successfully controverted, the book caused repercussions that forced him to leave England to escape trial for treason. He sought refuge in France. Almost immediately he became involved in the French Revolution as a staunch supporter of the revolutionary party. He boldly advocated the perpetual banishment of Louis XVI, but was opposed to the execution of the king. His tolerant views on this subject must have alienated the Terrorists, for Robespierre caused him to be imprisoned under sentence of death by the guillotine. It was just before this imprisonment that he published the first part of his immortal book, *Age of Reason;* he wrote the second part during the ten months of his incarceration.

Paine's escape from death in France was by one of those unforeseen circumstances which so often have changed the course of history. Robespierre fell from power. His successors restored Paine to his seat in the revolutionary convention.

When things in France had settled down to the sober process of setting up a permanent government, Paine turned his attention to George Washington, whom he bitterly attacked, thus losing much of his popularity in America.

Paine returned to the United States in 1802 and his closing years were comparatively uneventful. He died in 1809. Ten years later his body was sent back to England to be re-interred in his native earth.

Thomas Paine was a free thinker, a radical pamphleter. It was his misfortune to be "born out of time." Yet by his very birth and the energy of his nature he helped to change the face of time. He attacked the corruption of the British Government with such honesty and skill that he was the most feared man in England. Then, with the simple conviction of a Quaker Deist, he threw the power of his written word against the religious corruption that burdened the peoples of Europe and interfered with the social progress of mankind.

In the *Age of Reason,* Paine emphasized the necessity of separating the spheres of Church and State, looking at both institutions in their practical state of corruption rather than in their ideal state of mutual integrity. He held a broad view of religion in general, believing that all faiths were naturally good and were necessary to the spiritual security of humanity. Such broadness was out of season, and it made him numerous enemies among those holding fanatical convictions. It was dangerous to preach religious tolerance in his day, when the spirit of persecution was still strong.

When the clergy involved itself in the political conspiracies of the State and descended to the level of self-interest, their spiritual power was prostituted; and, said Paine, they lost all claim upon public respect. Paine saw the conniving, plotting, and counter plotting of religious leaders who had cast their lot with the aristocracy against long suffering and exploited citizens. With a Church such as this he had no patience, and he had the eloquence and abundant courage to express his convictions regardless of the cost.

He held the aristocracy in general in equal antipathy. Privileged classes, to him, were little better than parasites, living off the toil of honest men in total indifference to the public good. A government compounded from a dissolute nobility and fawning professional office holders, ever catering to the longer purse, brought Paine's righteous indignation to the boiling point, indignation which he could apply in words understandable to the masses. It was his simple reasoning that such a Church, plus such a State, equalled chaos. It was bad enough for government to burden the people with extravagances, but it was still worse for the Church to preach that men should accept this load as coming from God, to see it designed to purify their souls by the practice of patience and humility.

It was not enough for Paine to believe that all men were created free and equal; these free men had the inalienable right of representative government; and the further right to improve themselves to the enjoyment of all natural good.

He was more of a perfectionist than was practical in his own day or even in our time. Like most idealists, he failed to accept the weakness in that very human nature which he sought so desperately to champion. Only thousands of years of conditioning and the complete reorganization of government, religion, and education could bring mankind to the estate which Paine envisioned. He called men to a high destiny, and men understood in part and applied in part, but lacked the capacity for a full and understanding acceptance.

This probably explains Paine's bitter attack on George Washington. Paine had been present when the American government was formed, and he must have been at least a witness to the bickerings which went on during those most critical years. As a president, Washington was not universally popular; it was only after considerable engineering that his election had been accomplished. Almost immediately the new government fell into political difficulty. Self-seeking politicians appeared on the scene at the very beginning, just as they have never since been absent from the picture. Paine, seeing some of the noblest ideals of the new State perverted and misinterpreted, dared to speak when discretion held the tongues of other men.

In Paine's own public career, made up largely of reverses, he chose to accept all forms of personal humiliation rather than modify any of his attitudes. He never accepted that such a policy as he advocated would be impractical in a permanent form of government.

Political experience leads the wisest of public men to the realization that the possibilities of public office are limited, and that good things must be brought about slowly and opportunely if they are to survive public inertia and opposition. But in principle Paine was right, and he has left imperishable landmarks.

He was a Utopian, a dreamer with a mighty courage of conviction. And when the dream of world democracy is finally realized, Paine's name and memory will be immortalized; for he was outstanding among the great pioneers of human progress.

Thomas Paine's crusading was part of that secret destiny which has ordained that all people shall be free and equal.

Many times his career appeared to have been ended by the accidents of ill fortune, but always he was preserved against his enemies, and even against himself. He was one of the links in that golden chain which binds the earth to the pinnacle of high Olympus.

# 17

## THE UNKNOWN WHO SWAYED THE SIGNERS OF THE DECLARATION OF INDEPENDENCE

Faced with the death penalty for high treason, courageous men debated long before they picked up the quill pen to sign the parchment that declared the independence of the colonies from the mother country. For many hours they had debated in the State House at Philadelphia, with the lower chamber doors locked and a guard posted—when suddenly a voice rang out from the balcony. A burst of eloquence to the keynote, "God has given America to be free!" ended with the delegates rushing forward to sign. ...The American patriots then turned to express their gratitude to the unknown speaker. The speaker was not in the balcony; he was not to be found anywhere. How he entered and left the locked and guarded room is not known. No one knows to this day who he was.

OME years ago, while visiting the Theosophical colony at Ojai, California, A. P. Warrington, esoteric secretary of the society, discussed with me a number of historical curiosities, which led to examination of his rare old volume of early American political speeches of a date earlier than those preserved in the first volumes of the *Congressional Record*.

He made particular mention of a speech by an unknown man at the time of the signing of the Declaration of Independence. The particular book was not available at that moment, but Mr. Warrington offered to send me a copy of the speech, and he did; but unfortunately neglected to append the title or the date of the book. He went to India subsequently, and died at the Theosophical headquarters at Adyar, in Madras. Then, in May, 1938, the speech appeared in *The Theosophist,* official organ of the society published in Adyar. In all probability the original book is now in the library of the Theosophical society. There is no reason to doubt the accuracy and authenticity of Mr. Warrington's copy, but I am undertaking such investigation as is possible to discover the source of the speech.

On July 4, 1776, in the old State House in Philadelphia, a group of patriotic men were gathered for the solemn purpose of proclaiming the liberty of the American colonies. From the letters of Thomas Jefferson which are preserved in the Library of Congress, I have been able to gather considerable data concerning this portentous session.

In reconstructing the scene, it is well to remember that if the Revolutionary War failed every man who had signed the parchment then lying on the table would be subject to the penalty of death for high treason. It should also be remembered that the delegates representing the various colonies were not entirely of one mind as to the policies which should dominate the new nation.

There were several speeches. In the balcony patriotic citizens crowded all available space and listened attentively to the proceedings. Jefferson expressed himself with great vigor; and John Adams, of Boston, spoke and with great strength. The Philadelphia printer, Dr. Benjamin Franklin, quiet and calm as usual, spoke his mind with well chosen words. The delegates hovered between sympathy and uncertainty as the long hours of the summer day crept by, for life is sweet when there is danger of losing it. The lower doors were locked and a guard was posted to prevent interruption.

According to Jefferson, it was late in the afternoon before the delegates gathered their courage to the sticking point. The talk was about axes, scaffolds, and the gibbet, when suddenly a strong, bold voice sounded—"Gibbet! They may stretch our necks on all the gibbets in the land; they may turn every rock into a scaffold; every tree into a gallows; every home into a grave, and yet the words of that parchment can never die! They may pour our blood on a thousand scaffolds, and yet from every drop that dyes the axe a new champion of freedom will spring into birth! The British King may blot out the stars of God from the sky, but he cannot blot out His words written on that parchment there. The works of God may perish: His words never!

"The words of this declaration will live in the world long after our bones are dust. To the mechanic in his workshop they will speak hope: to the slave in the mines freedom: but to the coward kings, these words will speak in tones of warning they cannot choose but hear...

"Sign that parchment! Sign, if the next moment the gibbet's rope is about your neck! Sign, if the next minute this hall rings with the clash of falling axes! Sign, by all your hopes in life or death, as men, as husbands, as fathers, brothers, sign your names to the parchment, or be accursed forever! Sign, and not only for yourselves, but for all ages, for that parchment will be the textbook of freedom, the bible of the rights of man forever.

"Nay, do not start and whisper with surprise! It is truth, your own hearts witness it: God proclaims it. Look at this strange band of exiles and outcasts, suddenly transformed into a people; a handful of men, weak in arms, but mighty in God-like faith; nay, look at your recent achievements, your Bunker Hill, your Lexington, and then tell me, if you can, that God has not given America to be free!

"It is not given to our poor human intellect to climb to the skies, and to pierce the Council of the Almighty One. But methinks I stand among the awful clouds which veil the brightness of Jehovah's throne.

"Methinks I see the recording Angel come trembling up to that throne and speak his dread message. 'Father, the old world is baptized in blood. Father, look with one glance of Thine eternal eye, and behold evermore that terrible sight, man trodden beneath the oppressor's feet, nations lost in blood, murder, and superstition, walking hand in hand over the graves of the victims, and not a single voice of hope to man!'

"He stands there, the Angel, trembling with the record of human guilt. But hark! The voice of God speaks from out the awful cloud: 'Let there be light again! Tell my people, the poor and oppressed, to go out from the old world, from oppression and blood, and build My altar in the new.'

"As I live, my friends, I believe that to be His voice! Yes, were my soul trembling on the verge of eternity, were this hand freezing in death, were this voice choking in the last struggle, I would still, with the last impulse of that soul, with the last wave of that hand, with the last gasp of that voice, implore you to remember this truth—God has given America to be free!

"Yes, as I sank into the gloomy shadows of the grave, with my last faint whisper I would beg you to sign that parchment for the sake of those millions whose very breath is now hushed in intense expectation as they look up to you for the awful words: 'You are free.' "

The unknown speaker fell exhausted into his seat. The delegates, carried away by his enthusiasm, rushed forward. John Hancock scarcely had time to pen his bold signature before the quill was grasped by another. It was done.

The delegates turned to express their gratitude to the unknown speaker for his eloquent words.

He was not there.

Who was this strange man, who seemed to speak with a divine authority, whose solemn words gave courage to the doubters and sealed the destiny of the new nation?

Unfortunately, no one knows.

His name is not recorded; none of those present knew him; or if they did, not one acknowledged the acquaintance.

How he had entered into the locked and guarded room is not told, nor is there any record of the manner of his departure.

No one claimed to have seen him before, and there is no mention of him after this single episode. Only his imperishable speech bears witness to his presence.

There are many interesting implications in his words.

He speaks of the 'rights of man,' although Thomas Paine's book by that name was not published until thirteen years later.

He mentions the all-seeing eye of God which was afterwards to appear on the reverse of the Great Seal of the new nation.

In all, there is much to indicate that the unknown speaker was one of the agents of the secret Order, guarding and directing the destiny of America.

Some time ago, an eastern publisher suggested to me that an interesting and important title for a book would be, "The History of Unknown Men." This publisher was a great reader of history; and it was his observation that nearly all great causes are furthered by mysterious and obscure persons who receive little or no credit for the part which they have played.

To write the history of these men would be to write the history of the Order of the Quest, the story of the unknown philosophers. Some, like Francis Bacon, come to high estate; but most of the unknowns work obscurely through other men, who gain the credit and the fame.

In an old book of rules used by the brothers of the secret orders, is the following: "Our brothers shall wear the dress and practice the customs of those nations to which they travel so that they shall not be conspicuous or convey any appearance that is different or unusual. Under no condition shall they reveal their true identity, or the work which they have come to accomplish; but shall accomplish all things secretly and without violating the laws or statutes of the countries in which they work."

Of those who did not 'reveal their true identity', or the work which they came to accomplish, one is the mysterious Professor who inspired the design of our flag, and remains unknown and unnamed. And similarly, another is the unknown speaker whose words removed indecision about signing the Declaration of Independence; it is not known who he was, and the incident is preserved only in a rare old book, the very existence of which it is difficult to prove.

It is reasonably conceivable that in secrecy and anonymity well ordered aid has been given to the struggle for human equity and justice that has been America's destiny through the past into our present time. It is our duty and our privilege to contribute what we can to this Universal plan. It will go on, served by the unknowns, until the Platonic empire is established on the earth, and the towers of the new Atlantis rise from the ruins of a materialistic and selfish world.

# 18

## THE SYMBOLS OF THE GREAT SEAL
## OF THE U. S.

Is the American eagle actually a Phoenix? Selection of the
fabulous bird of the ancients seems to have been the
intention of the designer of our nation's Great Seal.
The Phoenix is the symbol of the Reborn in Wisdom....
The design on the reverse of the Great Seal is even more
definitely related to the Order of the Quest. The pyramid
and the all-seeing eye represent the Universal House surmounted by the radiant emblem of the Great Architect
of the Universe....These three symbols in combination
is more than chance or coincidence.

On the reverse of our nation's Great Seal is an unfinished pyramid to represent human society itself, imperfect and incomplete. Above floats the symbol of the esoteric orders, the radiant triangle with its all-seeing eye. Was it the society of the unknown philosophers who sealed the new nation with the ancient and eternal emblems?

HEN the time came to select an appropriate emblem for the great seal of the United States of America, several designs were submitted. These are described by Gaillard Hunt, in *The History of the Seal of the United States,* published in Washington, D. C., in 1909. Most of the designs originally submitted had the Phoenix bird on its nest of flames as the central motif. One of the designs now familiar to us was finally selected, and Benjamin Franklin was asked for his opinion of the choice.

Franklin gave his immediate approval, observing naively that it was very appropriate to select the wild turkey as the symbol of the new country: The turkey was a bird of admirable quality, hard working and industrious, and of good moral character, and a fowl also with a marked adversion for the color red, at that time unpopular among the colonists.

When it was explained to Franklin that the bird on the seal was intended to represent an eagle he was bitterly disappointed; and he insisted that the drawing did not look like an eagle to him, and furthermore, an eagle was a bird of prey with few of the respectable qualities of the wild turkey.

It has been said that the designer had drawn a Phoenix. Its selection would of course have been appropriate.

Among the ancients a fabulous bird called the Phoenix is described by early writers such as Clement, Herodotus, and Pliny; in size and shape it resembled the eagle, but with certain differences. The body of the Phoenix is one covered with glossy purple feathers, and the plumes in its tail are alternately blue and red. The head of the bird is light in color, and about its neck is a circlet of golden plumage. At the back of its head the Phoenix has a crest of feathers of brilliant color. Only one of these birds was supposed to live at a time, with its home in the distant parts of Arabia, in a nest of frankincense and myrrh. The Phoenix, it was said, lives for 500 years, and at its death its body opens and the new born Phoenix emerges. Because of this symbolism, the Phoenix is generally regarded as representing immortality and resurrection.

All symbols have their origin in something tangible, and the Phoenix is one sign of the secret orders of the ancient world and of the initiate of those orders, for it was common to refer to one who had been accepted into the temples as a man twice-born, or re-born. Wisdom confers a new life, and those who become wise are born again.

The Phoenix symbol is important in another way, as an emblem among nearly all civilized nations of royalty, power, superiority, and immortality. The Phoenix of China is identical in meaning with the Phoenix of Egypt; and the Phoenix of the Greeks is the same as the Thunder Bird of the American Indians.

In the accompanying drawing, the head of the bird as it appeared on the great seal of 1782 is compared with the present form. It is immediately evident that the bird on the original seal is not an eagle, nor even a wild turkey as Franklin had hoped, but the Phoenix, the ancient symbol of human aspiration toward Universal good. The beak is of a different shape, the neck is much longer, and the small tuft of hair at the back of the head leaves no doubt as to the artist's intention.

But if this design on the obverse side of the seal is stamped with the signature of the Order of the

Quest, the design on the reverse is even more definitely related to the old Mysteries.

Here is represented the great pyramid of Gizah, composed of 13 rows of masonry, showing 72 stones. The pyramid is without a cap stone, and above its upper platform floats a triangle containing the All-Seeing Eye surrounded by rays of light.

This design was not pleasing to Professor Charles Eliot Norton, of Harvard; he summed up his displeasure in the following words. "The device adopted by Congress is practically incapable of effective treatment; it can hardly (however artistically treated by the designer) look otherwise than as a dull emblem of a Masonic Fraternity." The quotation is from *The History of the Seal of the United States*.

If incapable of artistic treatment, the great seal is susceptible of profound interpretation. The Pyramid of Gizah was believed by the ancient Egyptians to be the shrine tomb of the god Hermes, or Thot, the personification of Universal Wisdom.

No trace has ever been found of the cap of the great pyramid. A flat platform about thirty feet square gives no indication that this part of the structure was ever otherwise finished; and this is appropriate, as the Pyramid represents human society itself, imperfect and incomplete. The structure's ascending converging angles and faces represent the common aspiration of humankind; above floats the symbol of the esoteric orders, the radiant triangle with its all-seeing eye. The triangle itself is in the shape of the Greek letter D, the Delta, the first letter of the name of God—the divine part of nature completing the works of men.

The 72 stones are the 72 arrangements of the Tetragrammaton, or the four-lettered name of God, in Hebrew. These four letters can be combined in 72 combinations, resulting in what is called the Shemhamforesh, which represents, in turn, the laws, powers, and energies of Nature by which the perfection of man is achieved.

The Pyramid then is the Universal house, and above its unfinished apex is the radiant emblem of the Great Architect of the Universe.

There is a legend that in the lost Atlantis stood a great university in which originated most of the arts and sciences of the present race. The University was in the form of an immense pyramid with many galleries and corridors, and on the top was an observatory for the study of the stars. This temple to the sciences in the old Atlantis is shadowed forth in the seal of the new Atlantis. Was it the society of the unknown philosophers who sealed the new nation with the eternal emblems, that all the nations might know the purpose for which the new country had been founded?

The obverse of the great seal has been used by the Department of State since 1782, but the reverse was not cut at that time because it was regarded as a symbol of a secret society and not the proper device for a sovereign State.  Quite rare are discoveries of the use of this symbol in any important form until recent years.  Most American citizens learned for the first time what was the design on the reverse of their seal when it appeared on the dollar bill, series of 1935A.

So far as anyone may know, the use of the seal in 1935 was probably without premeditation or special implication.  But it is interesting that its appearance should coincide with great changes affecting democracy in all parts of the world. As early as 1935 the long shadows of a world tyranny had extended themselves across the surface of the globe. Democracy was on the threshold of its most severe testing.  The rights of man, that Thomas Paine defended, were being assailed on every hand by selfishness, ambition, and tyranny.  Then on the common medium of our currency appeared the eternal emblem of our purpose.

The combination of the Phoenix, the pyramid, and the all-seeing eye is more than chance or coin-

cidence. There is nothing about the early struggles of the colonists to suggest such a selection to
farmers, shopkeepers, and country gentlemen.
There is only one possible origin for these symbols,
and that is the secret societies which came to this
country 150 years before the Revolutionary War.
Most of the patriots who achieved American independence belonged to these societies, and derived
their inspiration, courage, and high purpose from
the ancient teaching. There can be no question
that the great seal was directly inspired by these
orders of the human Quest, and that it set forth
the purpose for this nation as that purpose was
seen and known to the Founding Fathers.

The monogram of the new Atlantis reveals this
continent as set apart for the accomplishment of
the great work—here is to arise the pyramid of
human aspiration, the school of the secret sciences.
Over this nation rules the supreme king, the Ever
Living God. This nation is dedicated to the fulfillment of the Divine Will. To the degree that
men realize this, and dedicate themselves and their
works to this purpose, their land will flourish. To
depart from the symbol of this high destiny is to
be false to the great trust given as a priceless inheritance.

# 19

## THE PROPHETIC DREAM OF GENERAL MC CLELLAN

In a dark hour of military apprehension the General of the Union forces was visited by a vision in a dream. A voice spoke and a map came alive with troop movements as the enemy forces moved into the very positions he had intended to occupy. The voice told him that he had been betrayed; he raised his eyes and looked into the face of George Washington....When McClellan awoke his map was covered with marks and signs and figures, indicating the strategy that prevented the capture of the nation's Capitol....Also included in the dream was the warning of the Father of Our Country that we would wage still another struggle for existence "ere another century shall have gone by" against the "oppressors of the whole earth."

HE vision of Constantine changed the course of the Roman Empire. The visions of Joan of Arc preserved France in an hour of darkest need. And the vision that came to General McClellan was a powerful force in preserving the Union of the American people.

The story of General McClellan's dream, preserved in the General's own words, seems to have appeared in print for the first time in the Portland (Maine), *Evening Courier,* of March 8, 1862. Had the story not been true, it is almost certain that McClellan himself would have made some statement of disproval or demanded a retraction.

General McClellan's career as a soldier was not exceptionally brilliant; he was a good organizer,

but made many enemies because of certain fixa-
tions of temperament; but there can be no question of his sincerity and his dedication to the cause
of the Union.  In the interests of brevity here we
will give a digest of parts of the story of the dream,
with the General's own words preserved in the
more significant passages.

At two o'clock of the third night after General
McClellan's arrival at Washington, D. C., to take
command of the United States Army, he was
working over his maps and studying the reports
of scouts.  A feeling of intense weariness came
over him, and leaning his forehead on his folded
arm he fell asleep at his table.  He had not been
sleeping more than ten minutes when it seemed
that the locked door of his room was suddenly
thrown open, and someone strode up to him and
in a voice terrible with power spoke: "General
McClellan, do you sleep at your post?  Rouse
you, or ere it can be prevented, the foe will be in
Washington."

The General then describes in some detail his
strange feeling.  At the moment he seemed to
be suspended in the center of infinite space, and
the voice came from a hollow distance all about
him.  He started up, but whether he was really
awake he was never able to decide.  The table

covered with maps was still before him, but the furniture, the walls of the room, and other familiar objects were no longer visible.   Instead, he was gazing upon a living map including the entire area of the country from the Mississippi river to the Atlantic ocean.

McClellan tried to see the features of the being that stood with him, but could discern nothing but a vapor having the general outline of a man.

As he looked upon the great map, McClellan was amazed to see the movements of the various troops and regiments, and a complete pattern of the enemy's lines and distribution of forces.   The General was immediately infused with a great elation, for he felt that the movements on this extraordinary map would enable him to bring the war to a speedy and victorious termination.

Then his elation changed to great apprehension, he saw the enemy's forces moving to certain points which he himself had intended to occupy within the next few days.   He quietly realized that in some way his plans were known to the enemy.

Then again the voice spoke.   "General McClellan, you have been betrayed.   And had God not willed otherwise, ere the sun of tomorrow had set the Confederate flag would have waved above the

Capitol and your own grave. But note what you see. Your time is short."

His pencil moving with the speed of thought, McClellan transferred the troop positions from the living map to the paper map on his desk. When this had been done, McClellan became aware that the figure standing near him had increased in light and glory until it shone like the noonday sun. And as he raised his eyes he looked into the face of George Washington.

The first President with sublime and gentle dignity looked upon the bewildered officer, and spoke as follows: "General McClellan, while yet in the flesh I beheld the birth of the American Republic. It was indeed a hard and bloody one, but God's blessing was upon the nation and, therefore, through this, her first great struggle for existence, He sustained her and with His mighty hand brought her out triumphantly. A century has not passed since then, and yet the child Republic has taken her position of peer with nations whose pages of history extend for ages into the past. She has, since those dark days, by the favor of God, greatly prospered. And now, by very reason of this prosperity, has she been brought to her second great struggle. This is by far the most perilous ordeal she has to endure; passing as she is from childhood to opening maturity, she is called on to accomplish that vast result, self-conquest; to learn that important lesson, self-control, self rule, that in the future will place her in the van of power and civilization...

"But her mission will not then be finished; for ere *another century* shall have gone by, the oppressors of the whole earth, hating and envying her exaltation, shall join themselves together and raise up their hands against her. But if she still be found worthy of her high calling they shall surely be discomfitted, and then will be ended her *third* and last great struggle for existence. Thenceforth shall the Republic go on, increasing in power and goodness, until her borders shall end only in the remotest corners of the earth, and the whole earth shall beneath her shadowing wing become a Universal Republic. Let her in her prosperity, however, remember the Lord her God, her trust be always in Him, and she shall never be confounded."

As the spirit visitor ceased speaking he raised his hand over McClellan's head in blessing, and the next instant a peal of thunder rumbled through space. McClellan woke with a start. He was again in his room with his maps spread out on the table before him.

But there was one difference; the maps were covered with the marks, signs, and figures which he had inscribed there during the vision.

McClellan walked about the room to convince himself that he was really awake. He then returned and looked at the maps. The markings were still there.

Convinced now that the experience was heaven sent, McClellan had his horse saddled and rode from camp to camp making the necessary changes in his strategy to meet the enemy's planned offensive.

His moves were successful, and he prevented the capture of the city of Washington. At that time the Confederate Army was so close that Abraham Lincoln, sitting in his study at the White House, could hear the rumble of the Confederate artillery.

General McClellan concludes his account of the strange vision that saved the Union with these words: "Our beloved, glorious Washington shall again rest quietly, sweetly in his tomb, until perhaps the end of the Prophetic Century approaches that is to bring the Republic to a third and final struggle, when he may once more, laying aside the crements of Mount Vernon, become a Messenger of Succor and Peace from the Great Ruler, who has all the Nations of the Earth in his keeping.

"But the future is too vast for our comprehension; we are the children of the present. When peace shall again have folded her bright wings and settled upon our land, the strange, unearthly map marked while the Spirit eyes of Washington looked down, shall be preserved among American archives, as a precious reminder to the American nation of what in their second great struggle for existence, they owe to God and the Glorified Spirit of Washington. Verily the works of God are above the understanding of man!"

It is not difficult to understand how a man who has been granted so strange an experience should come to realize that a secret destiny is overshadowing the country for which he fought.

The prophetic import contained in the vision is now apparent, and as the entire account was published in 1862 there can be no doubt that we are in the presence of a genuine example of foreknowledge. It is now 80 years since Washington appeared to General McClellan, and within the century the powers of the earth have risen to destroy the concept of world democracy. America is in the vanguard of the democratic nations, seeking to preserve its heritage from the encroachments of totalitarian powers. Already it is obvious that in the postwar period of reconstruction America must become a leader of nations in the establishment of a commonwealth of peoples. The purpose for which we are created is revealing itself through the long processes of time, and that purpose is indeed our most sacred heritage.

It is written in the old books that when the brothers of the Quest desire to bring about changes in the mortal state they send messengers and strange dreams and mystic visions and, accomplish their purpose by revealing their will to the leaders of nations in sundry and curious ways. Whether we wish to believe that the spirits of the dead return to guide the living, or whether we choose to accept that man possesses faculties and powers which under great stress may bring his consciousness a little nearer to Universal Truth, one thing is certain: Men unaccustomed to the spiritual ways of life have received visions, and have heard voices, and by obeying these mysterious powers they have contributed to the progress and security of their fellow men.

# 20

## THE END OF THE QUEST

In America shall be erected a shrine to Universal Truth, as here arises the global democratic Commonwealth—the true wealth of all mankind, which is designed in the foundation that men shall abide together in peace and shall devote their energies to the common cause of discovery....The power of man lies in his dreams, his visions, and his ideals. This has been the common vision of man's necessity in the secret empire of the Brotherhood of the Quest, consecrated to fulfilling the destiny for which we in America were brought into being.

Religion, science, and philosophy are the three parts of essential learning. A government based upon one or even two of these parts must ultimately degenerate into a tyranny, either of men or opinion. These three realize the unity of knowledge; they are the orders of the Quest

HILOSOPHY teaches that the completion of the great work of social regeneration must be accomplished not in society but in man himself.

The democratic commonwealth can never be legislated into existence. Nor can it result from formal treaties or conferences. This is clearly indicated in the tragedy of the League of Nations. The League failed to prevent war because the nations which composed the League lacked the courage of high conviction; they failed the very institution which they themselves had established.

Permanent progress results from education, and not from legislation. The true purpose of education is to inform the mind in basic truths concerning conduct and the consequences of conduct. Education is not merely the fitting of the individual for the problems of economic survival. This is only the lesser part of learning.

The greater part deals with the intangibles of right motivation and right use. No human being who is moved to action through wrong motivations, or misuses the privileges of his times, can be regarded as educated, regardless of the amount of formal schooling he has received.

The human mind is established in knowledge not alone by the reading of books or the study of arts and sciences, but by the examples set up by leaders and the personal experiences of living. According to the Baconian system, there are three sources of learning. The first is tradition, which may be derived from books. The second is observation, by which we learn from the actions of each other. And the third is by experimentation, which is a study of causes and consequences brought about by personal conduct.

The supreme human purpose is the perfection of man. This must come first, and when this end has been achieved all good things will inevitably follow.

Only enlightened men can sustain enlightened leadership; only the wise can recognize and reward wisdom.

In a democratic way of life the very survival of the State depends upon the intelligent cooperation of its people. Where men make their own laws, they must live according to the merits and demerits of the statutes which they have framed.

The Greek law giver, Solon, declared that in the ideal State laws are few and simple, because they have been derived from certainties. In the corrupt State, laws are many and confused, because they have been derived from uncertainties. These corrupt laws are like the web of a spider which catches small insects but permits the stronger creatures to break through and escape.

Where there are many laws there is much lawlessness, and men come to despise and ridicule the restraints that are imposed upon freedom of action. Corrupt laws, resulting from efforts to amend inadequate legislation by further inadequate legislation, reveal a general ignorance of right and wrong. Where such ignorance exists the ideal function of democracy is impossible, and liberty degenerates into license.

The half-truth is the most dangerous form of lie, because it can be defended in part by incontestable logic. Wherever the body of learning is broken up, the fragments become partial truths. We live in a day of partial truths; and until we remedy the condition we must suffer the inevitable consequences of division.

According to the Ancients, religion, philosophy, and science are the three parts of essential learning. Not one of these parts is capable if separated from the rest, of assuring the security of the human state. A government based upon one or even two of these parts must ultimately degenerate into a tyranny, either of men or of opinion.

Religion is the spiritual part of learning, philosophy the mental part, and the sciences, including the arts and crafts, the physical part. As man himself has a spiritual, mental, and physical nature, and all of these natures manifest in his daily living, he must become equally informed in all the parts of his nature if he is to be self governing. "Unbalanced forces perish in the void," declared a prophet of old; and this is true beyond possibility of dispute.

The Platonic commonwealth had as its true foundation the unity of learning. In the midst of the philosophic empire stands the school of the three-fold truth. Religion is the quest of truth by means of the mystical powers latent in the consciousness of man. Philosophy is the quest for truth by the extension of the intellectual powers toward the substance of reality. Science is the quest for truth by the study of the anatomy and the physiology of the body of truth, as it is revealed in the material creation.

These three, then, are the orders of the Quest. Together they can bring about the perfection of man through the discovery of the Plan for man.

One of the great secrets of antiquity was this realization of the unity of knowledge and the identity of the Quest in all the branches of learning. The great philosophers of the past were truly great because they approached the problem of life as priest-philosopher-scientist. The title "The Wise" is properly applied only to those in whose consciousness the unity of knowledge has been established as the pattern of the Quest.

It was part of the ancient plan that has descended to us to build again the ideal university— the college of the six days work. Here would be taught the same arts and sciences that we teach today, but from a different basic premise. Here men would learn that the sciences are as sacred as the theologies, and the philosophies are as practical as the crafts and trades. Those mystical extra-sensory perceptions viewed with suspicion by the materialist would then be developed according to the disciplines of the sciences, and all learning would be consecrated to the supreme end that men become as the gods, knowing good and evil.

This university is the beginning of democratic empire. No longer would it be a secret school— the House of the Unkown Philosophers. It would emerge from the clouds which have concealed it from the profane for thousands of years and take its rightful place as the center and fountain-head of the Ever Living Good.

When humanity willfully ignores the Universal laws which govern its destiny, Nature has devious ways of pressing home its lessons. Civilization after civilization has been built up by human courage and destroyed by human ignorance. We stand again on the threshold of a great decision. Once more the workings of time have revealed the weaknesses of our social structure. Once more we have come to a day of reckoning.

In the postwar world one of two courses lies before us. Either we will make the old mistakes again, and try to force our own concepts upon the Universe; or we will gather our strength for one heroic effort to put things right.

If we make the old mistakes we will be rewarded by the old pain. But if we make the new effort, we can set up imperishable footings and bestow as a heritage the beginnings of a better way of life. According to our choice the results will be inevitable, for Nature will never change her ways. Let us consider her ways and be wise.

Centuries ago, one of the secret masters of the Quest wrote: "The Eternal Good reveals its will and pleasure through the body of Nature and the motions of Universal Law. Within the body of Nature and Law there is a soul which must be discovered by great thoughtfulness. And within that soul of Nature and Law there is a spirit which must be sought with great understanding; for verily I say unto you, my brothers, that it is this spirit concealed from the profane but revealed to the thoughtful, which giveth life."

This, then, is the design of our foundations: that men shall abide together in peace and shall devote their energies to the common cause of discovery.

Man is greater than the animal, not in strength of body, nor in shrewdness, nor in the power of his senses, nor even in skill and patience; man is superior because he contains within himself the faculties and powers by which he can perceive his true place in a divine order of life.

His power lies in his dreams, his visions, and his ideals. If these intangibles are left uncultivated, man is at best but a superior kind of beast, subject to all the ills and vicissitudes of an unenlightened creation.

But, as man has locked within him, hidden from the public gaze, this diviner part, so it is true that human society has within itself concealed from our common view a nobler part composed of the idealists and dreamers of all ages and of all races who have been bound together by their common vision of man's necessity. This is the secret empire of the poets, this is the order of the Unknown Philosophers, this is the Brotherhood of the Quest.

And never will these dreamers cease their silent working until that dream is perfected in our daily life. They are resolved that the Word which was made flesh shall become the Word made Soul.

The great Universtity of the Six Days Work must be built here in our Western world, to become a guide unto the nations. About this shrine to Universal Truth shall rise the democratic Commonwealth—the wealth of all mankind.

This is the destiny for which we were brought into being. The plan, which was devised in secrecy long ago, and in far places, shall be fulfilled openly ... as the greatest wonder born out of time.